THE POWER OF SELF-LOVE FOR TEEN GIRLS

7 SIMPLE TECHNIQUES TO FIGHT PEER PRESSURE, OVERCOME STRESS & ANXIETY, SET FIRM BOUNDARIES, AND EMPOWER YOURSELF

EMPOWERMENT PRESS

TABLE OF CONTENTS

INTRODUCTION

In the heart of every teen girl lies a unique journey, a path that weaves through the vibrant tapestry of emotions, challenges, and triumphs that define the adolescent years. It's a time brimming with potential yet often marked by an intense search for identity, acceptance, and meaning. This is where the transformative power of self-love becomes not just a practice but a beacon of light guiding you through the complexities of growing up. Through laughter and tears, successes and setbacks, self-love remains an unwavering source of strength and clarity.

This book is born from a vision to empower you to navigate the turbulent waters of peer pressure, overcome the shadows of stress and anxiety, set boundaries that honor your true self, and, most importantly, cultivate a relationship with yourself that's rooted in love and respect. While it's crafted with you at the forefront of every page, it also holds treasures for parents, teachers, or other support figures who wish to reinforce you on this journey.

What sets this guide apart is its commitment to speaking your language—clear, honest, and straight from the heart. We're not here to oversimplify your experiences or offer cookie-cutter solutions. Instead, we delve into the rich diversity of your stories, recognizing that self-love means different things to different people. This book is a tapestry of strategies, reflections, and exercises designed to meet you where you are and grow with you.

Sensitive topics? Absolutely, but it is approached with care, avoiding mature themes or romantic entanglements, focusing squarely on empowering you to build resilience, foster mental health, and embrace personal growth. Through interactive elements like journal prompts, motivational quotes, and real-life anecdotes, you'll find a space to explore, reflect, and celebrate your journey to self-love.

"Believe in yourself and all that you are. Know that there is something inside you that is greater than any obstacle." This affirmation echoes the spirit of our journey together—a journey of self-discovery, resilience, and empowerment. It's a journey that doesn't promise to be easy but assures that you're never alone.

Let me share a moment from my own life when the seeds of self-love were planted. I was in a situation where a difficult choice had to be made—one that couldn't wait yet would define my being, my worth, and my future. Standing at a crossroads, faced with the daunting task of making a decision that would alter the course of my life, it was the quiet voice of self-love that guided me. It whispered of my worth, reminding me that the choices I make should honor my values, dreams, and well-being. It was a defining moment of realization that self-love isn't just about feeling good—it's about making choices that reflect the deepest parts of who we are.

This book welcomes everyone, inviting you into a space where you're seen, heard, and valued for who you are and who you're becoming. Whether you're taking your first steps toward self-love or you're further along in your journey, there's a place for you here. Together, let's embark on this path of self-discovery and empowerment, embracing the power of self-love to transform our lives.

So, dear reader, with an open mind and heart, let's step forward into this journey—a journey not just of reading but of becoming the most authentic, loved, and empowered version of yourself.

THE ESSENCE OF SELF-LOVE

In the tapestry of life, every thread of experience, emotion, and thought weaves together to form the intricate pattern that is uniquely ours. Within this rich mosaic, one element stands out for its transformative power: self-love. It's not just a buzzword or a fleeting state of mind; it's the very soil from which the flowers of our lives grow. This chapter is dedicated to exploring self-love, not as a one-size-fits-all solution but as a deeply personal practice that shapes our reality, influences our choices, and colors our relationships.

1.1 DEFINING SELF-LOVE IN YOUR TERMS

The concept of self-love often brings to mind images of self-care routines or affirmations, yet its essence runs much deeper. It's akin to the process of nurturing a garden. Just as each plant requires specific care—the right amount of sunlight, water, and soil nutrients—self-love is similarly nuanced and individualized. It's about discovering and providing for your unique needs, preferences, and aspirations.

Personal Definition

Consider, for a moment, the vastness of the night sky. Each star shines with its own light, contributing to the beauty of the heavens. In much the same way, self-love illuminates our inner world, guiding us through a similar darkness. This illumination begins with crafting a personal definition of self-love; it's a definition that might evolve over time, shaped by experiences and reflections. For some, it means setting aside time for hobbies that ignite their passion; for others, it's about setting healthy boundaries in relationships. The key lies in understanding that there is no universal template for self-love, yet being brave enough to search deep within you for what allows your inner self to thrive. It's a personal creed—a set of principles tailored to your innermost needs and desires.

Self-Acceptance

At the heart of self-love lies self-acceptance. This is the *unwavering* acknowledgment of your worth, irrespective of achievements, appearance, or any external validation. It's the recognition that you are enough, just as you are. Self-acceptance does not mean complacency or refusal to grow; rather, it's about acknowledging your intrinsic value in the present moment. It involves embracing **every** aspect of yourself—the strengths and the vulnerabilities, the successes and the setbacks. This unconditional acceptance acts as a sanctuary, a place of solace and strength from which you can navigate life's challenges. It's in this place of peace that we can cater to our needs in order to continue growing.

Self-Compassion

Life, with its inevitable ups and downs, can sometimes feel like navigating a ship through stormy seas. In these moments, self-compassion is the lighthouse that guides us to safer waters. It's the gentle, understanding voice that reminds us that it's okay to be imperfect, to struggle, and to feel overwhelmed. Kristin Neff, a leading researcher on self-compassion, emphasizes its role in emotional resilience. By treating ourselves with kindness, understanding, and support, we bolster our ability to cope with life's stressors. Self-compassion involves recognizing that difficulties and failures are part of the human experience, allowing us to extend the same empathy and understanding to ourselves that we would offer a dear friend.

Setting the Foundation

Self-love lays the cornerstone for the edifice of our lives. It influences the paths we choose to follow, the relationships we cultivate, and the dreams we dare to pursue. When self-love is the foundation, we build our lives on a bedrock of authenticity and integrity. Decisions are made not out of fear or insecurity but from a place of strength and self-belief. Relationships flourish because they are chosen and nurtured from a place of worthiness and mutual respect. Dreams and aspirations are pursued with courage, fueled by the conviction that we are deserving of fulfillment and happiness.

In the practical realm, this might manifest in the choices we make daily—from the food we nourish our bodies with to the company we keep to the boundaries we set in our personal and professional lives. Each choice is a reflection of self-love, a testament to our commitment to honoring our well-being and happiness.

Remember that self-love is not a destination but a journey—one that is deeply personal and ever-evolving. It's a journey marked by moments of self-discovery, challenges that test our resolve, and victories that celebrate our resilience. And while the path may not always be smooth, the pursuit of self-love is one of the most rewarding journeys you can embark on. It's a journey that leads to a life lived with authenticity, purpose, and joy—a life where you are the author of your story, with you as the main character.

1.2 THE MYTH OF PERFECTION IN SOCIAL MEDIA

In today's digital age, social media platforms have transformed into a mirror reflecting a world where everyone seems to lead a perfect life except, perhaps, you. This mirror, however, distorts reality, often leaving us in a struggle with our self-image and self-worth. It's crucial to recognize that this digital realm, with its filters and highlight reels, can significantly skew our perception of what happiness and success really look like.

Unrealistic Standards

Scrolling through your feed, you encounter a barrage of images: flawless skin, picturesque vacations, and achievements celebrated with fanfare. These snapshots, while captivating, set a bar so high that they float in the realm of fantasy. The pressure to meet these unrealistic standards can be suffocating. It's like running a race with no finish line in sight—you push harder, yet the goalposts keep moving. Snippets of the lives of a fractionally small percentage of the population do not promote a healthy understanding of the world as a whole. Recognizing that these standards are not only unreasonable but also unnecessary is the first step toward freeing yourself from this relentless pursuit.

Comparison Trap

Falling into the trap of comparing your behind-the-scenes life to someone else's highlight reel is easy. You see the successes and joys of others, not the struggles and tears that precede them. This comparison can lead to a spiral of self-doubt and diminishing self-worth. Imagine if every flower in the garden compared itself to the others; the daisies would bemoan not being as tall as the sunflowers, and the roses would lament not blooming as early as the tulips. If the flowers were all the same, the garden would be bland and uninviting. It's their diversity that makes the garden beautiful. Similarly, embracing your unique journey and milestones is key to avoiding the pitfalls of comparison.

Authentic Self-Esteem

Building self-esteem on the shaky ground of likes, comments, and followers is like building a house on sand—it may stand for a while, but eventually, it will collapse under pressure. The storms of life will come, and the loose base of your self-esteem will be swept away in the floods of adversity. Authentic self-esteem is rooted in real achievements, personal growth, and qualities that go beyond the superficial. It's about celebrating small victories, like mastering a new skill or overcoming a fear and recognizing the attributes that make you uniquely you. Cultivating self-esteem from within ensures it remains unshakeable, even in the face of external fluctuations.

Navigating Social Media Healthily

In navigating the tricky waters of social media, setting a course toward healthier engagement can significantly impact your self-esteem and overall well-being.

- Curate Your Feed: Take control of the content you consume. Follow accounts that inspire, educate, and uplift you. If certain content triggers negative feelings, remember the unfollow button is your friend. Be brave and purposeful in removing influencers that don't contribute to your growth.
- Limit Screen Time: Designate specific times of the day for social media usage to prevent it from consuming your life. Use the extra time for activities that nourish your soul, like reading, spending time in nature, or engaging in hobbies that bring you joy. Adding variety to your day outside of your phone helps reset your worldview.
- Reality Check: Remind yourself that what you see online is a curated version of reality. For every perfect selfie, there were probably dozens of attempts. Behind every success story, there were challenges and setbacks. Keeping this perspective helps demystify the perfection seen online.
- Social Media Sabbaticals: Taking regular breaks from social media can be incredibly refreshing. It allows you to reconnect with yourself and the real world, appreciating life's simple pleasures without the urge to document or compare.
- Contribution over Consumption: Shift your focus from passive consumption to active contribution. Share content that reflects your real-life experiences, thoughts, and inspirations. Engaging authentically encourages others to do the same, fostering a more genuine online community. Taking a proactive stance in your digital circles allows for inspiration and encouragement from your own personal experiences to help others through their struggles.
- Mindful Engagement: Before scrolling, set an intention. Ask yourself, "What do I hope to gain from the time spent on social media?" Being mindful of your purpose can help

steer your engagement in a direction that supports your well-being. It helps you recognize reels or feeds that don't lend themselves to the purpose.

In a world where our digital and real-life personas intertwine, finding balance is key. Social media, when navigated wisely, can be a source of inspiration, connection, and learning. However, it's important to remember that it's just one facet of our lives. Our worth is not measured by the perfection of our online presence but by the richness of our real-world experiences and the depth of our character. By focusing on building authentic self-esteem and engaging with social media in a healthy, mindful way, we can enjoy the benefits of these platforms without falling prey to the pitfalls of comparison and unrealistic standards.

1.3 CELEBRATING YOUR UNIQUE JOURNEY

Every individual's life unfolds in its own time and manner, much like the aforementioned flowers in a garden bloom according to their own schedules. The beauty of embracing your distinctive path and recognizing the value of your experiences and the pace at which you grow is worth celebrating. It's an invitation to honor your personal narrative, with all its twists and turns, as a source of strength and self-love.

Embrace Individuality

Your individuality is what sets you apart, adding depth and color to the collective human experience. Your passions, dreams, quirks, and even the challenges you face contribute to the unique tapestry of your life. Embracing this individuality means recognizing your intrinsic value and the singular contributions you can make to the world. It's about standing firm in your authenticity, even when the currents of conformity threaten to sweep you away. Celebrate the aspects of yourself that break the mold, for it's in these differences that your true beauty shines.

Comparisons are Counterproductive

The act of comparing your life's path to that of others is akin to measuring the brightness of a candle against the sun—it's not only futile but dims the light you have to offer. Comparisons strip away the joy of the present, diverting attention from your achievements and growth. They foster a mindset of scarcity, overshadowing the abundance within and around you. Remember, the success of another does not signify your lack. Life is not a race or a competition but a canvas of individual stories, each with its own pace and rhythm. We can appreciate and celebrate each other's stories as we weave around one another. When you catch yourself in the trap of comparison, gently redirect your focus toward your progress and the steps you're taking on your own path.

Strength in Diversity

Imagine for a moment a world where every song sounded the same, every painting bore the same colors, and every story told the same tale. Such a world would lack the vibrancy and depth that diversity brings. Just as art, music, and literature are enriched by variety, so too is the human experience. The differences in our backgrounds, perspectives, and life experiences are not just to be tolerated but also celebrated. They offer fresh viewpoints, challenge our assumptions, and spur innovation and creativity. Embracing the diversity of human experiences broadens our understanding and fosters a world where every individual feels valued and heard. Recognize and celebrate the diversity within yourself and among those around you as a testament to the complexity and richness of life.

Celebration of Milestones

In the fast-paced rhythm of modern life, it's easy to gloss over the milestones that mark your personal growth and achievements. Yet, these moments, no matter how small they might seem, are the building blocks of your self-love journey. Celebrating these milestones serves as a reminder of your progress, reinforcing your sense of self-worth and accomplishment. It could be as simple as acknowledging the courage it took to express your opinion, the perseverance in overcoming a challenge, or the dedication to a project or cause. Each milestone is a testament to your strength, resilience, and growth.

Creating a ritual around celebrating these moments can amplify their significance. It might involve writing about the achievement in a journal, sharing the experience with a loved one, or treating yourself to something that brings you joy. Whatever form it takes, the act of celebration is a powerful affirmation of your worth and progress. It's a way to anchor yourself in the present, savoring the journey thus far while looking forward to the adventures that lie ahead. When we take the time to internally point out our successes, we're continuing to lay a stronger foundation of self-love.

As you navigate the winding paths of your life, remember that your pace, your struggles, and your victories are yours alone. They are not to be weighed against anyone else's but recognized and celebrated as integral parts of *your* story. In doing so, you cultivate a deep-seated sense of self-love and appreciation that fuels your journey forward with the knowledge that you are enough, just as you are.

1.4 THE IMPACT OF POSITIVE SELF-TALK

Language, in its essence, is the fabric of our thoughts and the architect of our reality. The words we whisper to ourselves in moments of doubt or triumph carry weight, molding our self-perception and, by extension, the world around us. Positive self-talk, then, acts as a tool that can sculpt a reality brimming with confidence, resilience, and self-compassion. It shifts the narrative from one of limitation to one of endless possibilities.

Power of Language

Consider for a moment the difference between the statements "I can't" and "I can learn." The former is a dead end, a barrier that halts progress. The latter, however, opens a door, inviting growth and exploration. This subtle shift in language embodies the transformative power of words. Positive self-talk fosters an environment where challenges are viewed not as insurmountable obstacles but as opportunities for growth. It nurtures a mindset where mistakes are not failures but stepping stones on the path to mastery. By consciously choosing words that affirm our capability and worth, we construct a self-image that is resilient, adaptable, and grounded in self-respect.

Changing the Narrative

The journey from negative to positive self-talk begins with awareness. It's about catching ourselves in the act of self-criticism and actively steering the conversation in a more compassionate direction. Here are a few techniques to facilitate this shift:

- Mindfulness: Practice mindfulness to become more aware of your internal dialogue. Begin to discover the root causes of your thoughts and feelings. This awareness is the first step in transforming negative thoughts.
- Question and Replace: When a negative thought surfaces, question its validity and replace it with a positive affirmation. For example, transform "I'm not good enough" into "I am capable of improving every day." The first thought will never be valid, and the second affirms your strength and character.
- Affirmation Cards: Create a set of affirmation cards with positive statements about yourself. Pull one out whenever you need a reminder of your worth and capabilities.
- Gratitude Journal: Maintain a gratitude journal, focusing on aspects of yourself and your life that you appreciate. Write about a kind word or a song that resonates with you. This practice shifts focus from what's lacking to what's abundant.

Self-Talk and Self-Esteem

The correlation between the quality of one's self-talk and the level of self-esteem is undeniable. When our internal dialogue is harsh and unforgiving, it erodes our sense of self-worth, leaving us feeling inadequate and unworthy. Conversely, when we speak to ourselves with kindness, understanding, and encouragement, our self-esteem flourishes. Positive self-talk reinforces our belief in our own value or worth, irrespective of external validation or achievement. It acts as an inner ally, championing our cause and reminding us of our inherent worth. This relationship underscores the importance of cultivating a positive internal dialogue, one that nurtures our self-esteem and supports our overall well-being.

Practical Exercises

To weave positive self-talk into the fabric of our daily lives, consider incorporating the following exercises into your routine:

- Morning Affirmations: Start your day with a set of affirmations that resonate with you. Speak them out loud, with conviction, in front of a mirror. This practice sets a positive tone for the day ahead.
- Journaling: Dedicate a few minutes each day to journaling about your varying experiences, however small. Reflect on what these experiences say about your character and capabilities.
- Self-Talk Monitor: Keep a self-talk monitor for a week. Note down instances of negative self-talk and how you reframed them into something positive. This actively trains your mind for question and replace strategies. Reviewing this log will highlight your progress and areas for further growth.
- Compliment Jar: Create a compliment jar where you deposit notes of self-praise or things you like about yourself. Reach into the jar for a boost whenever you're feeling low.

Incorporating these exercises into your life is not just about countering negative thoughts but about building a foundation of self-love and respect. It's about recognizing that the words we speak to ourselves shape our perceptions, influence our actions, and, ultimately, craft our reality. Positive self-talk is not merely an exercise in self-indulgence but a profound practice of self-care, one that acknowledges our worth and nurtures our growth. It's a testament to the belief that we are deserving of love, kindness, and respect, first and foremost from ourselves. Through this practice, we not only enhance our self-esteem but also empower ourselves to navigate the complexities of life with grace, resilience, and an unwavering belief in our own capabilities.

1.5 LEARNING TO APPRECIATE YOUR STRENGTHS

In the realm of self-love, recognizing and valuing your strengths and talents is akin to mastering a complex recipe. Each skill and quality you possess is a unique ingredient, contributing to the harmonious blend of flavors in your culinary creations. Yet, for many, these ingredients remain underutilized, lost amid the clutter of self-doubt and comparison. The following sections aim to guide you in identifying these hidden treasures, overcoming the barriers that obscure their true value, and crafting a dish that reflects the richness of your abilities.

Identifying Strengths

The first step in appreciating your strengths is to uncover them. This task can seem daunting, like searching for treasure without a map. However, with thoughtful reflection and a few guiding strategies, you can begin to unearth the gems that lie within.

- Reflection and Self-Assessment: Set aside time for quiet reflection. Consider moments when you felt most alive, fulfilled, or proud. Ask yourself what skills or qualities were at play during these times. Tools like personality tests and skill assessments can also offer insights into your natural talents and inclinations.
- Feedback from Others: Sometimes, those around us can see the strengths we overlook. Reach out to friends, family, and mentors. Ask them to share what they perceive as your strengths. Their observations can provide a new

perspective, highlighting abilities you may have undervalued or not recognized.

- Mark Successes in Your Journal: Start including callouts in your journal dedicated to tracking your achievements, no matter how small. Over time, patterns will emerge, revealing strengths you consistently draw upon to navigate challenges and accomplish goals.

Overcoming Impostor Syndrome

Impostor syndrome, the belief that you're not as competent as others perceive you to be, can cast a long shadow over your ability to recognize and appreciate your strengths. It whispers doubts, sowing seeds of disbelief in your accomplishments. Self-love is key to conquering imposter syndrome.

- Acknowledge the Feelings: Recognize when impostor syndrome surfaces. Acknowledging these feelings is the first step in addressing them. Understand that it's a common experience shared by many successful and capable individuals.
- Challenge Negative Thoughts: When you catch yourself doubting your abilities, challenge these thoughts. Ask yourself, "Is there evidence to support this belief?" More often than not, you'll find that your fears are not grounded in reality.
- Celebrate Your Achievements: Make a conscious effort to celebrate your achievements. Reflect on the hard work, skill, and perseverance that led to these successes. This practice reinforces your confidence in your abilities and counters the narrative impostor syndrome tries to impose.

Leveraging Strengths

Once you've identified your strengths, the next step is to weave them into the fabric of your daily life. By doing so, you not only enhance your personal growth and satisfaction but also enrich the lives of those around you.

- In School and Work: Look for opportunities to apply your strengths in academic or professional settings. Whether it's a knack for organizing, a talent for artistic expression, or a strength in analytical thinking, find ways to bring these abilities to the forefront. They can guide you toward subjects, projects, and careers where you can truly shine.
- In Hobbies and Interests: Align your hobbies and leisure activities with your strengths. This alignment not only increases enjoyment and fulfillment but also provides a space for your talents to flourish and evolve. Continue to expand your experiences as your recognition of the varying strengths grows.
- In Relationships: Your strengths can play a vital role in nurturing healthy relationships. For instance, if empathy and listening are among your strengths, they can enhance your ability to connect with and support friends and family. Be mindful of how your unique qualities can contribute to positive and meaningful interactions.

Gratitude for Abilities

Cultivating gratitude for your abilities transforms the way you view yourself and your place in the world. It shifts the focus from what you perceive as lacking to the abundance of talents and qualities you possess.

- Daily Gratitude Practice: Incorporate a daily practice of gratitude focused on your abilities. Each day, identify and express thanks for a skill, talent, or quality you appreciate in yourself. This practice not only bolsters self-esteem but also reinforces a positive self-image.
- Contribute to Others: One of the most profound ways to express gratitude for your abilities is to use them in service of others. Whether it's volunteering your time, sharing knowledge, or offering support, using your strengths to contribute to the community amplifies the sense of gratitude and fulfillment.
- Reflect on Growth: Regularly reflect on how your abilities have grown and evolved over time. Acknowledge the effort, experiences, and challenges that have shaped your development. This reflection fosters a deep appreciation for your journey and the strengths you've honed along the way.

As you move forward, remember that each of your strengths is a beacon, illuminating the road to self-discovery and fulfillment. By recognizing, valuing, and leveraging these gifts, you not only enrich your life but also bring light to those around you. Your abilities are not just assets to be appreciated but also tools to be actively used in crafting a life of purpose, joy, and self-love.

THE MINDFUL TEEN –
NAVIGATING LIFE WITH
AWARENESS

Picture this: Your mind is like a constantly buzzing phone, notifications popping up every second—homework, social drama, future worries. Now, imagine if there was a pause button, a way to quiet down the noise and just breathe. That's where mindfulness steps in, not as a trend but as your personal mental pause button, offering a way to navigate the urgency with a bit of calm.

Mindfulness might sound like something reserved for meditation retreats or yoga classes, but it's actually as simple and essential as breathing. It's about being here, in the now, fully experiencing this moment without judgment or distraction. For you, as a teen, it's a secret weapon against the pressures of growing up—a way to dial down the stress and tune into what really matters.

2.1 INTRODUCTION TO MINDFULNESS FOR TEENS

Mindfulness Explained

So, what exactly is mindfulness? At its core, mindfulness is paying full attention to what's happening, to what you're doing, and to the space you're moving through. That might seem trivial, except for the fact that we often veer from the matter at hand. Our minds take flight, we lose touch with our bodies, and soon we're engrossed in obsessive thoughts about something that just happened or fretting about the future. And that makes us anxious.

Yet no matter how far away we drift, mindfulness is right there to snap us back to where we are and what we're doing and feeling. If you're eating, it's about truly tasting that bite. If you're walking, it's feeling the ground under your feet. It's the realization that you don't have to be ruled by your emotions or caught up in thoughts about the past or future.

Starting Simple

Dipping your toes into mindfulness doesn't require hours of meditation. You can start simple.

- Breath Awareness: This is mindfulness at its most basic. Take a moment, wherever you are, to focus on your breathing. Notice the air moving in and out of your body, the rise and fall of your chest. It's about being present with each breath.
- Body Scans: Another beginner-friendly practice involves lying down and paying attention to different parts of your body. Start from your toes and work your way up, noticing

any tension or sensations. It's a way of connecting with your body and the present moment.

Mindfulness and Emotions

Our emotions can get the best of us, especially during our teen years, when everything feels magnified. Here's where mindfulness can really make a difference: It teaches us to observe our emotions without getting swept away. Angry about a comment someone made? Notice the anger without judgment and let it pass, like a cloud moving across the sky. The feeling of anger is valid, but it doesn't have to control you. Acknowledge the feeling and its source, learn from it, and let it go. By doing this, we can reduce the impact of negative feelings and react more calmly to situations.

Building a Routine

Making mindfulness part of your daily routine might seem like a tall order at first, but it's all about setting small, achievable goals. Here are a few tips:

- Set aside a few minutes each day: Start with just five minutes of mindfulness practice each morning or evening, and gradually increase the time.
- Use reminders: Post notes in places you'll see throughout the day or set alarms as a nudge to take mindful moments.
- Incorporate it into activities you already do: Brushing your teeth, eating breakfast, or walking to school can all become mindfulness practices with a shift in attention.

Practicing mindfulness doesn't mean changing who you are or stopping your thoughts. It's about observing them without getting caught up. The more you practice, the easier it gets to press that pause button on your buzzing mind, making space for peace and focus in your hectic life.

2.2 SIMPLE MINDFULNESS EXERCISES FOR DAILY ROUTINE

Incorporating mindfulness into your daily routine can transform ordinary moments into opportunities for awareness and growth. Here are some accessible exercises designed to infuse your day with mindfulness, enhancing your connection to the present moment and fostering a deeper appreciation for life's simple pleasures:

Mindful Mornings

Starting your day on a note of mindfulness can influence your mood and outlook for the hours ahead. Instead of reaching for your phone the moment you wake up, try this:

- Spend the first few minutes of your morning in silence, focusing on your breath. Notice the coolness of the air as you inhale and its warmth as you exhale.
- As you get ready, pay attention to each action, whether it's brushing your hair or getting ready for the day. Observe the sensations and movements, fully engaging with the process.
- Set an intention for the day. It could be something like, "Today, I will be kind to myself" or "I will focus on one task at a time." This helps direct your mind toward positive engagement throughout the day, giving you more control over potential threats to your well-being.

Mindful Eating

Mindful eating is about experiencing food more intensely—paying attention to the taste, textures, and sensations of eating. It's an effective way to improve your relationship with food and your body image by eating in response to physical hunger rather than emotional needs. Here's how to practice it:

- Before eating, take a moment to appreciate the food in front of you. Think about the journey it took to reach your plate. Acknowledge the effort that went into providing you with a meal.
- Chew slowly, savoring each bite. Try to identify all the different flavors and textures.
- Notice how your body feels as you eat. Are you starting to feel full? Are you eating because you're hungry, or is there another emotion at play?
- Put your utensils down between bites. This encourages you to slow down and truly enjoy your meal.

Mindful Movement

Incorporating mindful movement into your day is a wonderful way to connect with your body and appreciate its capabilities. Whether it's yoga, walking, or stretching, moving mindfully can enhance body awareness and promote physical and mental well-being. Here are a few tips:

- Choose a form of movement you enjoy. The more you enjoy it, the more likely you are to stay present. These types of movements are more likely to be incorporated into a routine.

- Focus on how your body feels as you move. Notice the stretch in your muscles, the rhythm of your breath, and any sensations of warmth or energy. You'll begin to notice how every part of your body works together to accomplish its tasks.
- If your mind wanders, gently bring your attention back to the movement and your breath. This practice is as much about building mental focus as it is about physical activity.

Mindful Breaks

Taking short, mindful breaks throughout your day can help reset and refocus your energy. These breaks are particularly beneficial during moments of stress or when you feel your attention waning. Here's how to make the most of these pauses:

- Step away from your work or study space to change your environment. This physical shift can help signal to your mind that it's time for a break. When you're deep into a study session, try to do this at least once an hour.
- Spend a few minutes focusing on your breath or engage in a quick mindfulness exercise, like noticing five things you can see, four things you can touch, three things you can hear, two things you can smell, and one thing you can taste. This gives your mind a quick shift from a focus topic, so it can come back refreshed and ready.
- Stretch your body. Gentle stretches can relieve physical tension and refresh your mind.
- Practice gratitude. Think of one thing you're thankful for at that moment. Gratitude shifts your focus to the positive, enriching your sense of well-being.

Integrating these exercises into your daily routine doesn't require a complete overhaul of your schedule or lifestyle. It's about making small, intentional changes that bring your focus back to the present, enriching your experience of the world around you. Tiny steps are the ones that get you moving in the right direction. Whether it's by starting your day with a moment of reflection, savoring your meals, moving with awareness, or pausing to breathe and stretch, each act of mindfulness is a step toward a more centered, peaceful, and fulfilling life.

2.3 MINDFULNESS IN THE AGE OF SOCIAL MEDIA

In an era where our digital footprints are as significant as our physical ones, mindfulness offers a fresh lens through which to view our interaction with social media. It's about fostering a relationship with these platforms that enriches, rather than detracts from, our mental and emotional well-being.

Digital Detox

The concept of a digital detox might initially seem daunting. The idea is not to cut out social media entirely but to take intentional breaks that allow you to recharge and refocus. Think of it as giving your mind a vacation from the constant influx of information and comparisons. These pauses can significantly lower stress levels and reduce feelings of inadequacy that often stem from relentless comparison. Start small—perhaps an hour before bed or the first hour after you wake up—and gradually increase the time. Notice the difference in how you feel during these periods. Many find they're more present, less anxious, and more attuned to their immediate environment and personal reflections.

Conscious Consumption

Mindful engagement with social media calls for conscious consumption. It's about being selective with what you absorb, choosing content that adds value, inspires, or educates. This approach necessitates an active role in curating your feed. Consume your digital content slowly and intently. Focus on the feelings and ideals that emanate from within you as you scroll. Then, follow accounts that mirror your interests and values or challenge you intellectually. Unfollow or mute those that stir feelings of inadequacy or discontent. By doing so, you transform your feed into a space that supports your well-being and reflects your aspirations.

Creating Mindful Content

Just as we aim to consume content mindfully, we can also strive to create and share with intention. This involves sharing moments or thoughts that genuinely resonate with you rather than posting for validation or to curate a certain image. Before sharing, ask yourself: Does this reflect my reality? Does it contribute positively to my digital community? Is it authentic to who I am? This approach not only cultivates a more genuine online presence but also encourages others to engage more authentically. By prioritizing mindfulness in both consumption and creation, we contribute to a more authentic, supportive online community.

2.4 THE POWER OF MINDFUL BREATHING

In a world that often feels like it's moving at lightning speed, finding an anchor can make all the difference. This anchor, surprisingly, lies within us—in the simple, rhythmic act of breathing. When we turn our attention to our breath, we tap into a powerful tool for bringing ourselves back to the moment, calming the chaos of our minds, and restoring balance to our emotions.

Breath Awareness

Imagine that each breath you take is a gentle wave washing over a beach. Just as the waves have a calming effect on the shore, focusing on your breath can have a similar soothing impact on your mind and body. This awareness acts as a bridge, connecting the mind and body and anchoring you firmly in the present moment. When you notice your thoughts beginning to spiral, directing your attention to the breath can act as a reset button, bringing immediate calm and a sense of presence. It's about noticing the air as it enters and exits your body, the way your chest rises and falls, and the subtle sensations of breathing.

Breathing Techniques

Several breathing techniques can be employed for different needs —be it stress relief, concentration, or emotional balance. Here are a few to explore:

- 4-7-8 Breathing: This technique involves inhaling for 4 seconds, holding the breath for 7 seconds, and exhaling for 8 seconds. It's particularly effective for reducing anxiety and helping with sleep.
- Square Breathing: Picture your breath traveling along a square. Inhale for 4 counts, hold for 4 counts, exhale for 4 counts, and hold again for 4 counts. This method is great for concentration and focus.
- Alternate Nostril Breathing: This involves covering one nostril, inhaling through the other, then covering the inhaling nostril and exhaling through the opposite nostril.

It helps balance the left and right sides of the brain, fostering emotional equilibrium and clarity of thought.

Integrating Breath Work

Incorporating mindful breathing into your daily activities can transform mundane tasks into moments of mindfulness. Here's how you can weave breath work into various aspects of your life:

- During Homework: Before you start your homework, take a few moments to practice a breathing technique. This can help clear your mind and increase focus, making it easier to tackle your assignments.
- In Sports: Use breath awareness to enhance performance and concentration in sports. Focusing on your breath can help you stay present, improve endurance, and reduce the likelihood of injury by keeping you attuned to your body's signals.
- While Being Creative: Prior to engaging in any creative activity, whether it's writing, drawing, or playing music, a few minutes of mindful breathing can open up the channels of creativity, allowing your inspiration to flow more freely.

The Science of Breathing

Understanding the physiological effects of controlled breathing can deepen your appreciation for this practice. When we engage in deep, mindful breathing, it signals to our body that it's time to relax, activating the parasympathetic nervous system. This counteracts the stress response triggered by the sympathetic nervous system, leading to a decrease in heart rate, a reduction in blood pressure, and a lowering of cortisol levels—the stress hormone.

Furthermore, mindful breathing enhances oxygen exchange, improves energy levels, and promotes a state of mental clarity and calm. Scientific studies have shown that regular practice of mindful breathing can have long-term benefits for mental health, including reduced symptoms of anxiety and depression, making it a potent tool for emotional well-being.

In essence, the act of directing our focus to our breath, something so fundamental yet often overlooked, can unlock profound benefits for our mental, emotional, and physical health. It serves as a reminder that sometimes, the most powerful resources we have are those that exist within us. By incorporating mindful breathing into our daily lives, we not only cultivate a deeper sense of calm and presence but also empower ourselves to navigate the complexities of life with a greater sense of ease and balance.

2.5 CULTIVATING GRATITUDE AS A MINDFULNESS PRACTICE

The practice of gratitude, simple in its essence, serves as a powerful reminder of the beauty and abundance that surround us, often hidden beneath the surface of our daily routines and challenges. By embracing gratitude, we not only sharpen our awareness of the present moment but also foster a deeper appreciation for the experiences that shape our lives.

Gratitude and Well-Being

The bond between gratitude and well-being is both profound and reciprocal. Engaging in gratitude brings our attention to the positive aspects of our lives, nurturing a sense of contentment and joy. This shift in focus naturally enhances mindfulness as we become more attuned to the richness of the present moment. Studies have shown that individuals who regularly practice gratitude report higher levels of happiness, lower stress, and a stronger sense of connection to others. Gratitude acts as a catalyst, transforming our perception of the world from one of scarcity to one of abundance.

Keeping a Gratitude Journal

One effective way to cultivate gratitude is through maintaining a gratitude journal. This practice involves dedicating a few moments each day to reflect on and record experiences, people, or aspects of your life for which you are thankful. Here are some tips to get started:

- Choose a Special Notebook: Select a journal that resonates with you, making the act of writing a more personal and enjoyable experience.
- Set Aside Time: Dedicate a specific time each day for your gratitude practice. Whether it's in the morning to start your day with positivity or in the evening as a reflective exercise, consistency is key.
- Be Specific: Instead of broad statements, try to focus on specific details. For instance, rather than writing, "I'm grateful for my friends," you might note, "I'm grateful for the laughter and support I shared with Jamie today."
- Reflect on Challenges: Consider including difficult situations and what they taught you or how they helped you grow. This can deepen your understanding and appreciation of life's complexities.

Gratitude in Relationships

Expressing gratitude within our relationships can profoundly impact the depth and quality of our connections. It's about acknowledging the value of others in our lives, recognizing their contributions, and voicing our appreciation. This practice not only strengthens bonds but also fosters an environment of mutual respect and kindness. Try these approaches:

- Direct Expressions of Thanks: Don't hesitate to express your gratitude directly, whether through words, a note, or a small gesture. Letting someone know you appreciate them can brighten their day and reinforce the positive dynamics in your relationship.
- Active Listening: Show your gratitude through the gift of your attention. Active listening, where you fully engage with what the other person is saying without distraction, is a powerful way to demonstrate your appreciation for their presence in your life.
- Acts of Kindness: Small acts of kindness can be a beautiful way to convey gratitude. Whether it's doing a favor without being asked or offering support during challenging times, these gestures can significantly impact the well-being of both the giver and the receiver.

Daily Gratitude Exercises

Incorporating gratitude into your daily routine can be both simple and transformative. Here are a few exercises to weave this practice into your day:

- Gratitude Walks: Take a walk where the sole intention is to notice and appreciate the beauty around you. It could be the warmth of the sun, the sound of birds, or the sight of trees swaying in the breeze.
- Thank-You Notes: Make a habit of sending thank-you notes, not just for gifts or grand gestures, but for the

everyday acts of kindness you witness or receive. This not only spreads joy but also reinforces your own practice of gratitude.

- Gratitude Jar: Create a gratitude jar where you deposit notes of things you're thankful for each day. Watching the jar fill up can be a visual reminder of the abundance in your life.
- Mindful Appreciation: Take a moment before meals to express gratitude for the food, considering the effort and resources that went into its preparation. This can turn a routine act into a mindful practice of appreciation.

By integrating these practices into our lives, we open ourselves to a more mindful and joyful existence, enriched by a deep sense of gratitude for the world around us and the people within it. Gratitude, in its essence, becomes a bridge to a more connected and fulfilling life, reminding us of the beauty that exists in the present and the abundance that flows from appreciating what we have.

As we wrap up this exploration of gratitude and its role in mindfulness, we carry forward the awareness that the simple act of giving thanks can profoundly impact our well-being, relationships, and overall outlook on life. With this foundation of mindfulness and gratitude, we are better equipped to navigate the complexities of our daily lives, anchored in the present and open to the richness of each moment. Now, as we turn our attention to the next chapter, we continue our journey, enriched by the practices we've explored and ready to embrace new insights and strategies for cultivating a life of mindfulness and joy.

STANDING TALL – YOUR VOICE AGAINST THE CROWD

I magine you're at a concert, surrounded by a sea of people. The music's pulsing through the air, but instead of losing yourself in the rhythm, you're acutely aware of how different you feel in your choice of attire, your lack of enthusiasm for the headlining band, or maybe even your decision to stay sober when everyone around you seems to be doing the opposite. It's like standing in the middle of a forest where every tree looks the same, and there you are—a stark, vibrant flower, questioning if you belong. This feeling is more common than you think, and it's a breeding ground for peer pressure. But here's the thing—being that flower amongst the trees is not just okay; it's beautiful. This chapter is about recognizing that beauty, standing in your truth, and navigating the sometimes murky waters of peer pressure with your head held high.

3.1 IDENTIFYING AND RESISTING PEER PRESSURE

Recognizing Peer Pressure

Peer pressure isn't always as obvious as someone daring you to do something you're uncomfortable with. It can be subtle—like feeling compelled to dress a certain way to fit in or laughing along at a joke you find offensive because you don't want to be the odd one out. It shows up in those moments when you're scrolling through your social media feed and suddenly feel the urge to buy something you don't need just because everyone seems to have it. It's in the silence that follows when you choose not to participate in gossip, and you can almost hear the whispers questioning your loyalty to the group.

Signs to Watch For: Notice when you're doing something that doesn't align with your values or when you're feeling uncomfortable with a group's decision but go along with it anyway. It's often in these moments that peer pressure is at work.

Inner Strength

What is the best shield against peer pressure? Your own inner strength, rooted in self-love. It's about knowing who you are, what you stand for, and where you draw the line. This doesn't mean you'll never have doubts or feel the urge to fit in, but it does mean you have a solid foundation to return to when those feelings arise.

Building Your Foundation: Spend time alone and get to know your likes, dislikes, values, and boundaries. It's like getting to know a friend—you can't stand up for them if you don't truly know them. The same goes for yourself.

Assertiveness Skills

Assertiveness is your voice in action. It's how you communicate your needs, preferences, and boundaries respectfully but firmly. Being assertive doesn't mean you're being rude or aggressive. It's about being honest and clear without stepping on anyone else's toes.

Strategies for Assertiveness: Practice saying "I feel" statements. Instead of "You're making me uncomfortable," try "I feel uncomfortable when …" This shifts the focus to your feelings rather than placing blame, making it easier for others to hear you without becoming defensive.

Role Models and Mentors

Role models and mentors can be guides through the fog of peer pressure. They're people who've navigated these waters before and can offer guidance, support, and sometimes, a much-needed reality check. They remind us that it's possible to stand firm in who we are, even when it feels like the world is pushing us to conform.

Finding Your Role Models: Look for individuals, whether in your personal life, history, or even characters in books or movies, who embody the kind of strength and integrity you aspire to. Reach out to teachers, family members, or community leaders who can offer mentorship and advice. Be open to their experiences and hardships so you can learn from them.

In the face of peer pressure, remember, it's not just about resisting something—it's about standing for something. It's about honoring your values, embracing your individuality, and choosing actions that align with your true self. It's not always easy, but it's always worth it.

3.2 STORIES OF TEENS WHO STOOD THEIR GROUND

In a world where the pressure to conform can feel overwhelming, there are stories of young individuals who have stood firm, rooted in their values and emerged stronger. These tales not only serve as beacons of hope but also offer valuable lessons on navigating the complexities of adolescence with integrity. Let's explore some of these narratives, drawing out the wisdom they offer.

Inspirational Narratives

Meet Alex, a high school sophomore who found themselves at a crossroads when their group of friends decided to skip class to attend a party. The excitement was palpable, but so was Alex's discomfort. The thought of breaking the rules for a moment of fun didn't sit right with them. After much internal debate, Alex chose to stay behind, facing the ridicule of their peers head-on. This decision wasn't easy, especially when photos of the party flooded social media, accompanied by mocking comments directed at Alex. However, standing by their decision fostered a deep sense of self-respect within Alex, a feeling far outweighing the temporary allure of the party.

Then there's Jordan, an avid basketball player who often found themselves on the fringes of their team due to a refusal to partake in the hazing of new members—a tradition that felt cruel and unnecessary. Despite the isolation and being labeled as "too soft," Jordan remained steadfast in their belief that respect and team-work were paramount to a true sportsman's spirit. This conviction eventually won over several teammates, leading to a shift in how new players were welcomed, making the team stronger and more united.

Learning from Experience

From Alex and Jordan, several key insights emerge:

- Resilience: Facing peer pressure head-on strengthens your resolve and fosters resilience, a quality that will serve you well beyond your teenage years.
- Courage: It takes immense courage to stand alone, to be the sole voice of dissent in a chorus of conformity. This courage is a testament to your character.
- Self-Respect: The pride that comes from staying true to yourself is incomparable. It builds a foundation of self-respect that influences future decisions and interactions.

Community Support

Finding support from like-minded individuals or groups can be a lifeline when standing against peer pressure. After their decision to stay behind, Alex discovered a club at school dedicated to volunteer work—an interest they'd always harbored but never pursued due to fear of judgment. This new community not only offered support but also a sense of belonging and purpose that Alex had long sought.

Jordan, on the other hand, found solace in an online forum for athletes who advocate for positive team cultures. This virtual community provided a space to share experiences, strategies for dealing with hazing, and encouragement. The realization that they were not alone in their beliefs was empowering.

- Seeking Support: Don't underestimate the power of finding your tribe—those who share your values and offer support when you choose to stand your ground.
- Expanding Horizons: Often, standing firm against peer pressure opens doors to new opportunities and communities that align more closely with your authentic self.

Empowerment through Reflection

Reflecting on the stories of Alex and Jordan, consider moments in your life when you've faced similar crossroads. Think about the emotions that surfaced, the choices you made, and the outcomes that followed. Reflecting on these experiences can be a powerful exercise in understanding and reinforcing your values.

- Identify Your Values: What principles guided your decisions? Recognizing these can clarify your core values.
- Evaluate the Outcomes: Consider the short-term and long-term effects of your choices. Often, the benefits of staying true to yourself far outweigh the temporary discomfort of going against the grain.
- Acknowledge Your Growth: Every act of resistance against peer pressure is a step toward personal growth. It's a chance to reaffirm your values and strengthen your sense of self.

In sharing and reflecting on these stories, we find a common thread—the undeniable strength that comes from knowing who you are and standing firm in that knowledge, even when faced with opposition. These narratives not only inspire but also serve as a roadmap for navigating the challenges of peer pressure with grace and conviction. Through the lens of these experiences, we see the transformative power of resilience, courage, and unwavering belief in oneself.

3.3 BUILDING A SUPPORT SYSTEM FOR EMPOWERMENT

Navigating the complexities of adolescence requires more than just personal resolve; it often demands a network of supportive relationships that encourage and uplift us. This network, or support system, becomes our safety net, catching us when we falter and boosting us toward our goals.

Choosing Friends Wisely

Making friends who echo our values and respect our journey toward self-love is akin to choosing teammates for a relay race. Each person plays a crucial role in reaching the finish line. When selecting friends, it's beneficial to look beyond surface-level commonalities and assess deeper connections. Do they respect your choices, even when they diverge from the group? Are they there for you during challenging times? Friends who encourage you to grow rather than hold you back are the ones who add real value to your life.

- Engage in activities or clubs that align with your interests. These spaces often attract individuals with similar values and passions.
- Observe how potential friends react to differences of opinion or conflicts. Their response can offer insights into their character and how they might support you in times of need.
- Trust your instincts. Sometimes, our gut feelings can guide us toward the right people.

Family as Allies

Our families can be our first line of defense against the pressures of the world. They can provide a foundation of love and acceptance, but this doesn't mean navigating family dynamics is always straightforward. Open communication is key. Share your feelings, aspirations, and the challenges you're facing with your family. When they understand your perspective, they're better equipped to offer the support you need.

- Schedule regular check-ins with family members to share updates about your life and hear about theirs. This habit fosters mutual understanding and support.
- When facing peer pressure, discuss specific instances with your family. They can offer advice based on their experiences or simply provide a listening ear.
- Recognize that support can sometimes mean giving you space to make your own decisions. Express to your family how this form of support is just as valuable.

Finding Like-Minded Communities

Beyond our immediate circles, there's immense power in connecting with broader communities that share our values and interests. Whether these communities are found online or in person, they offer a sense of belonging and a collective strength that can reinforce our personal resolve.

- Research clubs, organizations, or online forums that focus on areas you're passionate about. These can range from environmental advocacy groups to book clubs, offering not just camaraderie but also avenues for personal growth.

- Participate actively once you join these communities. Sharing your experiences and listening to others can deepen your sense of connection and mutual support.
- Use these communities as a sounding board. Discussing decisions or challenges with people who understand your perspective can provide valuable insights and encouragement.

The Role of Self-Love Groups

Amid the vast landscape of communities and support networks, self-love groups hold a special place. These groups, dedicated to the practice and promotion of self-love and empowerment, offer a sanctuary for individuals fighting against peer pressure and societal expectations.

- Look for local or online self-love groups. Many such communities organize regular meet-ups, workshops, or discussion forums focused on building self-esteem, practicing self-care, and supporting personal growth.
- Share your journey and listen to others. The stories and strategies shared within these groups can offer comfort, inspiration, and practical advice for overcoming common challenges.
- Engage with the resources provided by these groups. Many offer access to articles, videos, and other materials that can enrich your understanding and practice of self-love.

In every step of our path toward self-empowerment, the people we surround ourselves with play a pivotal role. They influence our thoughts, impact our decisions, and shape our perceptions of ourselves and the world. By consciously choosing friends who uplift us, leveraging our family relationships for support, connecting with like-minded communities, and participating in self-love groups, we weave a safety net that not only catches us when we fall but also propels us toward our highest potential. This network, built on the foundations of mutual respect, understanding, and shared values, becomes an indispensable source of strength and empowerment. Through these connections, we find the encouragement to remain true to ourselves, resist peer pressure, and continue on our journey with confidence and resilience.

3.4 SETTING BOUNDARIES WITH FRIENDS

Navigating the waves of friendship, especially during the teenage years, can sometimes feel like steering a boat through uncharted waters. It's thrilling yet daunting, filled with moments of both discovery and challenge. One of the skills that can turn these voyages into rewarding journeys is understanding how to set and communicate boundaries. It's about knowing where your personal space begins and ends and, more importantly, ensuring that those around you respect it.

Understanding Boundaries

Boundaries are invisible lines that delineate what we are comfortable with and what we are not in terms of our personal space, emotions, and physical well-being. They are essential for maintaining a sense of self-respect and self-love, acting as safeguards that protect our well-being. When we set boundaries, we communicate to others how we expect to be treated—what is acceptable and what is not. This clarity helps prevent misunderstandings and ensures that our relationships are built on mutual respect and understanding.

- Emotional Boundaries: These involve your feelings and how you choose to share them, for instance, deciding with whom you share personal information.
- Physical Boundaries: These relate to your personal space and physical touch. Everyone has different levels of comfort, and it's important that friends respect these preferences.
- Time Boundaries: This involves how you choose to spend your time and with whom. It's about balancing different aspects of your life without feeling overwhelmed or taken advantage of.

Communicating Boundaries

The key to setting boundaries is clear and respectful communication. It's about expressing your needs and limits in a way that's assertive yet considerate. Here are some tips to effectively communicate your boundaries:

- Be Direct and Clear: Use simple, straightforward language. Instead of hinting or hoping your friend will guess your limits, explicitly state them.
- Use "I" Statements: Frame your boundaries in terms of your own needs and feelings. For example, "I feel uncomfortable when we talk about this topic. Can we discuss something else?"
- Be Consistent: Consistency reinforces your boundaries. If you're firm about a limit one day but lax about it the next, it sends mixed signals.
- Practice: If you're not used to asserting your boundaries, practice what you want to say ahead of time. It can help you feel more confident when the time comes.

Respecting Others' Boundaries

Just as we want our boundaries to be respected, it's crucial to extend the same courtesy to others. Respecting someone's boundaries shows that you value their comfort and well-being. It fosters a healthy dynamic where both parties feel safe and valued. Pay attention to verbal and nonverbal cues that might indicate you're crossing a line, and always ask if you're unsure. Remember, a friendship built on mutual respect is one that's likely to last and thrive.

- Ask Questions: If you're uncertain about a friend's limits, ask them. It's better to have a clear understanding than to assume.
- Apologize if You Cross a Boundary: We all make mistakes. If you inadvertently cross a friend's boundary, apologize sincerely and learn from the experience.
- Encourage Open Communication: Make it known that you're open to discussing boundaries. This can help create an environment where both of you feel comfortable expressing your needs.

Dealing with Boundary Violations

Even with the best intentions, there may be times when friends cross your boundaries. Handling these situations requires tact and assertiveness.

- Address the Issue Promptly with Your Friend: If a boundary is crossed, address it directly with your friend as soon as possible. Don't gossip about the situation to another friend while you're upset or hurt. The longer you wait, the harder it may become to speak up.

- Express How the Violation Affected You: Let your friend know how their actions impacted you. For example, "When you shared that story about me with others, I felt embarrassed and betrayed."
- Reiterate Your Boundary: Clearly restate your boundary. It's possible your friend didn't fully understand it the first time.
- Consider the Relationship: If boundary violations are a recurring issue, it might be time to reassess the friendship. Relationships should enhance your life, not detract from it.

In instances where you feel your safety or well-being is at risk, don't hesitate to seek help from a trusted adult or professional. Remember, setting and respecting boundaries is not about creating distance but about building relationships that are healthy, respectful, and enriching. It's a skill that, once honed, will serve you well throughout your life, ensuring that your journey through the complexities of friendship is both rewarding and respectful.

3.5 CONFIDENCE IN SAYING "NO"

The tiny word "no" holds immense power. It can shape your life's path, safeguard your peace, and reflect your deepest values. Yet, for something so small, it's often one of the hardest words to say. The reluctance stems from various places—fear of disappointing others, worry about being perceived as unkind, or even the dread of missing out. However, learning to say "no" is a critical skill, a gatekeeper of your well-being.

The Power of "No"

Saying "no" is a declaration of independence. It announces to the world—and, more importantly, to yourself—that you are the captain of your ship. When choices loom, and you're faced with options that don't align with your core values or threaten your well-being, saying "no" keeps you true to your course. It's a form of self-respect, a way to honor your needs, limits, and desires.

Consequences of Not Saying "No"

Failing to voice a "no" when needed can lead down a slippery slope. Initially, it might seem like you're keeping the peace, avoiding conflict, or just being helpful. Over time, however, the toll becomes apparent. Stress builds as you take on more than you can handle. Resentment brews, not just toward those who keep asking but toward yourself for not standing firm. Relationships may suffer, not thrive, as they become one-sided. Recognizing these consequences highlights the importance of saying "no" as an act of self-care.

Role-Playing Scenarios

One effective way to grow comfortable with saying "no" is through role-playing. This exercise can prepare you for real-life situations, reducing the anxiety associated with standing your ground.

- Scenario Planning: With a friend or family member, outline scenarios where you typically struggle to say "no." These could range from requests to participate in activities you're not comfortable with to pressures to conform to behaviors misaligned with your values.
- Role Reversal: Take turns playing both roles—the person making the request and the one declining. This perspective shift can offer insights into the dynamics at play and help you understand the other person's likely responses.

- Develop Responses: Craft and practice responses that are clear, concise, and respectful. Phrases like "I appreciate you thinking of me, but I can't commit to that right now" offer a polite yet firm refusal.

Self-Love as the Foundation

At its core, the capacity to say "no" springs from self-love and self-respect. It's a recognition of your worth, an acknowledgment that your mental and emotional health are paramount. Saying "no" is not selfish; it's a necessary boundary that enables you to engage with the world on your terms. It allows you to conserve your energy for the commitments and people that truly matter—those that align with your values and contribute positively to your life.

In nurturing this foundation of self-love, remember:

- Reflect on Your Values: Understanding what truly matters to you makes it easier to identify when something doesn't align with those values.
- Prioritize Your Well-Being: Recognize that your mental, emotional, and physical health should always take precedence. Saying "no" to protect these is not just your right but your responsibility.
- Practice Self-Compassion: Be kind to yourself as you navigate the complexities of asserting your boundaries. It's a skill that takes time to develop.

In embracing the power of "no," you open the door to more authentic engagements, relationships based on mutual respect, and opportunities that truly resonate with your soul. It's a skill that not only enhances your well-being but also deepens your connection to your values and aspirations.

As we close this chapter, let's carry with us the understanding that saying "no" is an essential aspect of self-care, an affirmation of our values, and a declaration of our autonomy. It's a practice that, though challenging, rewards us with greater freedom, peace, and alignment with our true selves. It prepares us to step into the next phase of our journey with confidence, equipped with the knowledge that we have the strength to make choices that honor our well-being and aspirations.

MANAGING THE MAZE – STRATEGIES FOR STRESS AND ANXIETY

P icture this: You're in a maze. The walls are high, the paths are convoluted, and every turn seems to bring you face-to-face with a new challenge. This maze isn't made of hedges or stone; it's crafted from the stress and anxiety that come with being a teen today. From navigating academic pressures to decoding the complex social dynamics of high school and the daunting question of your future, it feels like you're constantly trying to find your way through.

Yet, what if I told you that within you lies the power to not just navigate this maze but to transform it into a landscape of learning and growth? This chapter delves into understanding stress and its impact on you, highlighting how self-love can be your map, guiding you through anxiety with confidence and resilience.

4.1 UNDERSTANDING STRESS AND ITS IMPACT

Stress in Adolescence

For teens, stress sources are as varied as they are vast. Academic pressures top the list, with the need to maintain grades, prepare for college, and choose a career path weighing heavily. Then there's the social arena—navigating friendships, dealing with bullying or social media stressors, and perhaps even facing challenges at home. Future uncertainties only add to this mix, creating a cocktail of stress that's all too common among today's youth.

Physical and Mental Effects

Stress and anxiety don't just live in the mind; they manifest in the body, too. Maybe you've felt your heart race before a test or experienced a stomach ache during a confrontation. These are your body's responses to stress. Mentally, the effects can range from trouble concentrating and making decisions to feelings of overwhelm. Chronic stress can lead to more serious issues like depression and anxiety disorders. Recognizing these signs early on is crucial for managing stress effectively.

Self-Love vs. Stress

Amid this, self-love acts as a buffer. It's about treating yourself with the same kindness and understanding you'd offer a friend in distress. Self-love encourages positive self-talk, reminding you of your strengths and abilities when you're drowning in doubt. It's about giving yourself permission to take breaks, to say no, and to prioritize your well-being. This doesn't mean stress disappears, but self-love equips you with a healthier perspective on how to face it.

Early Intervention

Catching stress early and taking steps to manage it can prevent it from escalating into more significant issues. This means paying attention to your body and mind, recognizing when you're starting to feel overwhelmed and taking action. Maybe it's talking to a counselor, practicing mindfulness, or simply taking a day off to recharge. Early intervention is about acknowledging that it's okay to ask for help and taking the steps to get the support you need.

Techniques for Stress Management

While understanding stress is the first step, actively managing it requires a set of strategies tailored to your lifestyle and needs. Here are some practical ways to deal with stress and anxiety:

- Exercise: Physical activity is a proven stress reliever. It doesn't have to be intense; a simple walk, dance session, or yoga can significantly impact your mood.
- Connect with Others: Spending time with friends or family or even engaging in social activities can provide a much-needed distraction and support network.
- Limit Screen Time: Reducing the time spent on electronic devices, especially social media, can lower stress levels and improve sleep.
- Mindfulness and Meditation: Practices like mindfulness and meditation can help calm your mind, bringing your focus back to the present and reducing anxiety.

- Time Management: Organizing your tasks and setting realistic deadlines can help manage academic pressures and reduce the feeling of being overwhelmed.
- Creative Outlets: Channeling your emotions through art, music, writing, or any creative activity can be an effective way to express and understand your feelings.

When to Seek Professional Help

While these strategies are effective for managing everyday stress, there are times when professional help may be needed. If you find yourself feeling persistently sad, anxious, or overwhelmed, and these feelings are interfering with your daily life, reaching out to a mental health professional is a crucial step. Remember, seeking help is a sign of strength, not weakness. It's about taking care of yourself and ensuring you have the support you need to navigate life's challenges.

In navigating the maze of adolescence, understanding and managing stress is key to maintaining your mental and emotional well-being. By recognizing the signs of stress early, employing effective coping strategies, and embracing self-love, you equip yourself with the tools to not only navigate but thrive in the face of challenges. Remember, you're not alone in this journey, and support is always available, whether from loved ones or professionals.

4.2 SELF-CARE STRATEGIES FOR BUSY TEENS

In a world where the clock seems to tick faster, carving out time for self-care can feel like trying to hold water in your hands—elusive and fleeting. Yet, the secret lies not in finding more time but in weaving self-care into the fabric of your daily life. Here, we discover strategies that fit snugly into the bustling schedules of teens, ensuring that self-care becomes as natural as breathing.

Practical Self-Care

Self-care doesn't require grand gestures or hours of free time. It's the small, everyday actions that count. Consider these manageable practices:

- Five-Minute Morning Rituals: Start your day with a brief activity that centers you—be it jotting down three things you're grateful for, stretching, or savoring a favorite scent or flavor. This sets a positive tone for the day ahead.
- Technology Time-Outs: Implement short, regular intervals where you step away from screens. These moments can be filled with quick walks, doodling, or simply sitting quietly, allowing your mind a much-needed break.
- Audio Relaxation: Use music or guided meditations available through apps or online platforms. Listening during your commute or while doing chores can effortlessly incorporate relaxation into your routine.
- Hydration and Snacks: Keeping a water bottle and healthy snacks on hand ensures you're fueling your body and brain, even when on the move.

Prioritizing Self-Care

Amid deadlines and commitments, self-care often slides to the bottom of the to-do list. Elevating its priority means reshaping our perspective to view self-care not as a luxury but as a necessity.

- Nonnegotiable Time Slots: Assign specific times in your schedule for self-care, treating them with the same importance as any other appointment or class.
- Communicate Your Needs: Be open with friends and family about your self-care practices. When they understand its importance to you, they're more likely to support you in maintaining these habits.
- Self-Care Buddy: Partner with a friend to keep each other accountable for daily self-care. Having someone to share the journey with can make the process more enjoyable and consistent.

Self-Care Plan

A personalized self-care plan acts as a roadmap, guiding you through the choices and practices that best support your well-being. Crafting this plan involves:

- Identify Stressors and Joys: Pinpoint what aspects of your life drain your energy and which ones replenish it. This awareness is crucial to tailoring your self-care practices.
- Set Clear, Achievable Goals: Whether it's ensuring eight hours of sleep each night, dedicating 15 minutes a day to reading for pleasure, or practicing deep breathing exercises during breaks, define what self-care looks like for you.
- Flexibility Is Key: Allow your plan to be flexible. Some days might be too packed for your usual self-care routine, so having shorter, alternative practices can keep you on track without adding stress.

Self-Care and Productivity

The myth that self-care is somehow opposed to productivity persists, yet the truth is that they're deeply interconnected. Shattering this myth begins with understanding:

- Enhanced Focus and Energy: Regular self-care recharges your batteries, so to speak, leading to increased focus and energy. It's easier to tackle tasks efficiently when you're not running on empty.
- Stress Reduction: Self-care practices, especially those centered around relaxation and mindfulness, can significantly lower stress levels, making it easier to manage responsibilities and challenges.
- Creative Thinking: Engaging in self-care activities that you enjoy can spark creativity. A relaxed mind is more likely to think outside the box and come up with innovative solutions.

Incorporating self-care into your life as a busy teen doesn't mean overhauling your schedule or making grandiose plans. It's about acknowledging the little ways you can nurture your well-being amid the hustle and bustle. It's recognizing that taking care of yourself isn't a detour from your responsibilities but a pathway that leads to a more balanced, joyful, and productive life.

4.3 THE ROLE OF PHYSICAL ACTIVITY IN REDUCING ANXIETY

When we move our bodies, something magical happens on a biochemical level. Engaging in physical activity isn't just about keeping the body fit; it's a catalyst for releasing endorphins, those feel-good chemicals that act like natural painkillers and mood elevators. This process is akin to lighting a candle in a dim room, gradually filling the space with warmth and light. As these endorphins flood our system, they mitigate stress and dissipate the clouds of anxiety, offering a sense of tranquility and an improved mood.

Exercise and Endorphins

Imagine your body as a complex chemical laboratory. When you exercise, it's as if you're initiating a positive chemical reaction. Physical activity prompts your brain to ramp up the production of endorphins. These chemicals, often referred to as the body's "feel-good neurotransmitters," play a pivotal role in reducing pain and boosting pleasure, resulting in a feeling of well-being. This doesn't mean you need to engage in intense workouts to reap the benefits. Even moderate, regular exercise can trigger this endorphin release, helping to lighten your mood and fend off anxiety.

Finding Enjoyable Activities

The key to making exercise a consistent part of your life is to find activities that bring you joy. It's less about the intensity or the calories burned and more about how it makes you feel. When you enjoy the activity, it doesn't feel like a chore; instead, it becomes something you look forward to.

- Explore Different Options: From dancing in your room to hiking in nature, cycling around the neighborhood, or even practicing martial arts, the possibilities are endless. Experiment with various activities until you find the ones that resonate with you.
- Social Exercise: Sometimes, exercising with friends can add an extra layer of enjoyment. Whether it's a friendly

game of basketball or a dance class, socializing while moving can make the experience more fulfilling.

- Set Realistic Goals: Rather than aiming for perfection or comparing your performance to others, focus on personal progress and the joy of movement. Celebrating small achievements will motivate you to stay on track.

Incorporating Movement into Daily Life

For those who aren't naturally inclined toward athletic pursuits, integrating more movement into daily routines can serve as a gentle introduction to a more active lifestyle.

- Active Commuting: Consider walking or biking to school or the store instead of riding in a car. These small changes can significantly increase your daily physical activity.
- Take the Stairs: Opting for the stairs instead of the elevator is a simple way to work more exercise into your day.
- Active Breaks: Use breaks between study sessions or during commercials to stretch, do some jumping jacks, or take a brief walk. These moments of activity can refresh both your mind and body.

Mind-Body Connection

The synergy between physical health and mental well-being cannot be overstated. When we take care of our bodies, our minds reap the rewards. This mind-body connection underscores the holistic impact of exercise on our overall health.

- Stress Release: Physical activity serves as an outlet for stress. It provides a physical means to expel the tension that accumulates in our bodies due to anxiety or stress.

- Improved Sleep: Regular exercise can contribute to more restful sleep patterns. Better sleep not only aids in stress reduction but also supports cognitive functioning and mood regulation.
- Enhanced Self-Esteem: As you meet fitness goals, even small ones, your self-esteem gets a boost. This newfound confidence can spill over into other areas of your life, creating a positive feedback loop that further diminishes anxiety.

In essence, the act of moving our bodies extends far beyond the physical benefits. It's a powerful tool for maintaining mental health, managing anxiety, and fostering a sense of well-being. By finding joy in movement, weaving more activity into our daily lives, and nurturing the connection between our physical and mental health, we open the door to a more balanced, serene state of mind.

4.4 NUTRITIONAL SELF-CARE FOR MENTAL WELL-BEING

The relationship between what we eat and how we feel is much like the connection between the quality of soil and the health of a garden. Just as fertile ground nourishes plants, enabling them to flourish and bloom, a balanced diet can significantly enrich our mental health, providing a stable foundation for managing stress and anxiety. In this light, considering the role of nutrition in our overall well-being becomes not just a matter of physical health but a vital component of mental care.

Food and Mood

The concept that our diet influences our mood extends beyond the temporary satisfaction of consuming our favorite foods. Scientific research suggests that certain nutrients have the power to modify brain chemistry, influencing our emotions and stress responses. For instance:

- Omega-3 Fatty Acids: Found in fish like salmon and in flaxseeds, these fats are linked to decreased rates of depression and anxiety.
- Complex Carbohydrates: Foods such as whole grains release glucose slowly, helping to maintain steady energy levels and mood.
- Proteins: Rich in amino acids, proteins from sources like turkey, eggs, and beans aid in the production of neurotransmitters like serotonin, which promotes feelings of well-being.

Incorporating a variety of these nutrients into your diet can help stabilize your mood, making you better equipped to handle stress.

Hydration and Health

Often overlooked in discussions about nutrition and mental health is the simple act of staying hydrated. Water is essential for every cell in our body, including brain cells. Dehydration can lead to difficulties in concentrating, increased irritability, and heightened levels of stress. Here are a few tips for maintaining proper hydration:

- Keep a Water Bottle Handy: Having water within reach encourages regular sips throughout the day rather than waiting until you're thirsty.
- Flavor Your Water: If plain water doesn't appeal to you, try adding slices of fruits like lemon, cucumber, or berries for a natural flavor boost.
- Eat Water-Rich Foods: Incorporate fruits and vegetables with high water content, such as watermelon, cucumber, and oranges, into your meals and snacks.

Mindful Eating

Revisiting the practice of mindful eating offers another avenue through which nutrition can support mental well-being. This approach encourages a deeper connection with the act of eating, focusing on the experience rather than on external distractions or emotional triggers. Here's how to apply mindful eating principles to reduce stress and anxiety:

- Eat Slowly: Take the time to chew thoroughly and savor each bite, allowing yourself to fully experience the flavors and textures.
- Listen to Your Body: Tune into your body's hunger and fullness cues. Eating in response to physical need rather than emotional desire fosters a healthier relationship with food.
- Appreciate Your Food: Reflect on the journey your food took to reach your plate, from the people involved in its production to the ingredients' growth and harvesting. This gratitude can transform eating from a mundane task into a meaningful ritual.

Simple Nutritional Changes

Adopting a diet that supports mental health doesn't have to be overwhelming. Small, incremental changes can have a significant impact:

- Incorporate a Rainbow of Fruits and Vegetables: Aim to include a variety of colors in your diet. Each color represents different nutrients and antioxidants that support brain health.
- Choose Whole over Processed: Whenever possible, opt for whole foods. These are closer to their natural state and typically contain more beneficial nutrients than their processed counterparts.
- Plan Your Meals: Taking the time to plan meals can help ensure a balanced diet. It also reduces the stress of last-minute decisions and the temptation of less healthy options.

By embracing these nutritional strategies, you're not just feeding your body; you're nourishing your mind. This holistic approach to eating acknowledges the intricate ways in which diet, mental health, and stress are intertwined. Simple choices, from what we put on our plates to how we engage with the act of eating, can serve as powerful tools for enhancing our mental well-being, helping us to navigate life's challenges with greater ease and resilience.

4.5 SLEEP HYGIENE AND ITS IMPORTANCE FOR TEENS

Navigating the complex world of adolescence, sleep often takes a back seat amid a whirlwind of assignments, extracurriculars, and social commitments. Yet, the silent guardian of our mental and physical well-being, sleep, holds the keys to emotional balance, sharp cognition, and overall vitality. Understanding its critical role can inspire a commitment to nurturing sleep, transforming it from a neglected necessity to a cherished ritual.

The Role of Sleep

Diving into the essence of sleep reveals its profound impact on our daily functioning. It's during these quiet hours that the brain processes the day's learning, consolidating memories and making sense of emotions. A lack of sufficient sleep disrupts this delicate balance, leading to heightened emotional reactivity and diminished cognitive abilities. In essence, skimping on sleep is like trying to navigate your day with a foggy lens—everything feels a bit more challenging and out of focus.

Common Sleep Challenges

Today's teens face a unique set of obstacles when it comes to securing a good night's rest. The lure of late-night scrolling on smartphones introduces not just distractions but also exposes us to blue light, which tricks our brains into thinking it's still daylight, disrupting the natural sleep-wake cycle. Coupled with erratic schedules that swing between late-night study sessions and early morning classes, establishing a consistent sleep routine seems like an uphill battle.

Developing Healthy Sleep Habits

Creating an environment and routine conducive to sleep can be likened to crafting the perfect bedtime story; it's personal, comforting, and leads to a peaceful end. Consider these steps to enhance your sleep hygiene:

- Establish a Consistent Routine: Aim to go to bed and wake up at the same time every day, even on weekends. This regularity trains your body's internal clock to expect sleep at a certain hour, making it easier to drift off.
- Create a Pre-Sleep Ritual: Engage in calming activities before bed to signal to your body that it's time to wind down. This could be reading a book, listening to soothing music, or practicing gentle stretches.
- Optimize Your Sleep Environment: Ensure your bedroom is a sanctuary for sleep. Keep it cool, dark, and quiet. Consider blackout curtains, eye masks, or white noise machines if needed. When possible, refrain from doing activities other than sleeping in your bed. This lets your body know and recognize that your bed is the place for sleep and nothing else.
- Limit Screen Time: Power down electronic devices at least an hour before bed. The blue light emitted by screens can inhibit the production of melatonin, the hormone that cues your body to go to sleep.

Sleep as Self-Care

Embracing sleep as a foundational pillar of self-care invites a shift in perspective from viewing sleep as a mere biological necessity to recognizing it as a vital source of rejuvenation and resilience. It's a time when the body repairs itself, the mind finds solace, and the spirit regains its energy. Prioritizing sleep is a profound act of self-love, acknowledging that to give your best to the world, you must first tend to your own needs.

This commitment to restorative sleep not only equips you to face the challenges of adolescence with grace but also lays the groundwork for lifelong well-being. It fosters a resilience that buffers against the stresses of daily life, ensuring that no matter the maze's complexity, you have the clarity, energy, and emotional equilibrium to navigate it successfully.

As we wrap up this exploration of the intricate dance between sleep and well-being, it becomes evident that nurturing our sleep is not just a personal endeavor but a critical investment in our future. It's an acknowledgment that to thrive, not merely survive, in the dynamic landscape of adolescence, we must honor our body's need for rest, allowing us to awaken each day with renewed purpose and vitality. By embracing these practices, we set the stage for a life marked by emotional richness, mental clarity, and boundless energy, ready to step into the next chapter of our journey with anticipation and an open heart.

HEALTHY RELATIONSHIPS –
REFLECTING YOUR INNER LOVE

Imagine your life as a symphony. Every relationship in it is like a unique instrument, each with its own melody and rhythm. Just as a conductor understands the significance of each instrument and how to orchestrate them, understanding how self-love influences your relationships helps you harmonize them and create a captivating symphony. This chapter guides you through composing a rich and expressive symphony of relationships, reflecting the notes of self-love, and creating a masterpiece that is both resonant and timeless.

Foundation of Friendships

Think of the last time you felt genuinely understood and supported by a friend. That connection likely wasn't random; it was built on a foundation where both of you respect and cherish each other for who you truly are. This foundation begins with you —knowing, accepting, and loving yourself sets the stage for the kinds of friendships that offer real support and joy. Like attracts like; when you radiate self-love, you naturally attract people who are also on their own paths of positive self-regard.

Real-Life Application: Start by dedicating time each week to activities that boost your self-awareness and self-esteem. Whether it's solo hikes that give you space to reflect or journaling about your dreams and challenges, these practices deepen your self-love, preparing you to attract and build healthier friendships.

Attracting Like-Minded Individuals

When you're confident in who you are, and you love yourself, you send out a vibe that's hard to ignore. It acts like a magnet for others who value the same qualities in themselves and their friendships. These are the people who will cheer on your successes, empathize with your struggles, and encourage your growth, all because they operate from a similar place of self-love and respect.

What to Look For: Pay attention to the people who make you feel more alive, understood, and valued. These are the individuals who reflect the positive aspects of your own self-love back at you.

Friendship Red Flags

Not all plants in your garden will be healthy; some might show signs of distress, indicating they're not thriving in the current environment. Similarly, some friendships can show red flags that signal a lack of mutual respect or support. These can range from constantly feeling drained after spending time with them to noticing a one-sided dynamic where your needs and feelings are often overlooked.

Signs to Watch Out For

- Frequent negativity or criticism that leaves you feeling insecure or undervalued.
- A lack of support or interest in your personal growth and achievements.
- Feeling pressured to change who you are to fit the friendship.

Nurturing Friendships

Healthy friendships, much like oft-played instruments, require regular care to be their best. This involves open communication, mutual support, and a willingness to invest time and energy into the relationship. It's important to apply the same qualities you're looking for in your relationships to how you treat your friends. It also means recognizing when a friendship is no longer reciprocal and making the tough decision to let it go, allowing more room for relationships that do support your well-being.

Strategies for Growth

- Regular Check-Ins: Make it a habit to regularly ask how your friend is doing and share your own experiences. This keeps the lines of communication open and strengthens your bond.
- Shared Experiences: Find activities that both of you enjoy and make plans to do them together. It could be as simple as trying out a new cafe or as adventurous as signing up for a dance class.
- Supportive Actions: Show up for them during both the good times and the bad. Celebrate their successes and offer

a listening ear or a shoulder to lean on when they're facing challenges.

Reflection Exercise

Take a moment to reflect on your current friendships. Consider the following questions:

- Do these relationships reflect the level of self-love and respect I hold for myself or want to hold for myself?
- Are there friendships that consistently leave me feeling drained or undervalued?
- How can I actively nurture the friendships that support my well-being?

Recording your thoughts in a journal can provide clarity and guide you in making decisions that align with your journey toward healthy, fulfilling relationships.

In navigating the symphony of relationships, the love and respect you cultivate for yourself set the tone for the connections you build with others. By choosing to nurture friendships that reflect your inner love, you enrich your life with meaningful, supportive bonds. Remember, in the symphony of existence, you are both the conductor and the melody.

5.2 COMMUNICATING YOUR NEEDS EFFECTIVELY

In the rich tapestry of relationships, the threads of communication weave patterns of understanding, connection, and mutual respect. It's through these threads that our needs, desires, and boundaries become known, making effective communication not just a skill but a cornerstone of healthy relationships.

Assertive Communication

At the heart of expressing ourselves lies the principle of assertive communication. This is about sharing our thoughts and feelings in a way that's both clear and considerate. It bridges the gap between passive silence and aggressive outspokenness, allowing us to stand our ground respectfully.

- Clarity Is Key: Begin by knowing exactly what you need to convey. This clarity ensures your message isn't lost in a sea of words or ambiguity. Take some time to make sure that your thoughts are in order before speaking your mind.
- "I" Statements: Use sentences that start with "I" to own your feelings and avoid blaming the other person. For example, "I feel upset when plans are canceled at the last minute" offers a personal perspective without pointing fingers.
- Respectful Tone: The tone of your voice can build connecting bridges or isolating walls. Aim for a calm and steady tone, even when discussing emotionally charged subjects.
- Compromise: Sometimes, meeting halfway can reinforce a relationship's foundation. Show a willingness to find a middle ground where both parties feel heard and valued.

Listening Skills

Active listening is the other half of the communication coin, equally vital but often overlooked. It involves fully engaging with the other person's words, showing empathy, and providing feedback that acknowledges their perspective.

- Full Attention: Give the speaker your undivided attention. This means setting aside distractions like phones or other tasks.
- Nonverbal Cues: Your body language speaks volumes. Nodding, maintaining eye contact, and leaning slightly forward can signal that you're fully present.
- Reflect Back: Summarize what you've heard in your own words. This not only shows you've been listening but also clarifies any misunderstandings.
- Empathy: Try to understand the emotions behind the words. Responding with empathy can deepen the connection and open doors to more meaningful conversations.

Conflict Resolution

Even in the most harmonious relationships, conflicts are inevitable. They're not signs of failure but opportunities for growth, provided we navigate them with care and respect for each other's needs and boundaries.

- Address Issues Early: Don't let small grievances pile up. Tackling issues when they're small can prevent them from growing into bigger problems.
- Focus on the Problem, Not the Person: Keep the conversation centered on the issue at hand rather than personal attacks. This keeps the path to resolution clear of unnecessary hurt.
- Listen for Underlying Needs: Often, conflicts stem from unmet needs. By listening attentively, you might uncover the real issue, paving the way for a solution that addresses the root cause.

- Agree to Disagree: Sometimes, agreeing to disagree is the most respectful resolution. It acknowledges that, while you may not see eye to eye, the relationship's value transcends differences.

Through the lens of assertive communication, active listening, and thoughtful conflict resolution, we can navigate the complexities of our relationships with grace. It's about creating a space where our needs and boundaries are respected, where we feel heard and valued, and where every conversation, no matter how tough, strengthens the bonds we share with those around us.

5.3 RECOGNIZING TOXIC RELATIONSHIPS

Identifying the signs of unhealthy relationships is akin to recognizing dissonant notes within a symphony. At first, listen, they may blend in, masquerading as harmonious melodies, but upon closer examination, their disruptive nature becomes apparent. Toxic relationships, like these dissonant notes, can diminish the overall quality of the symphony, marring the potential for joy and vibrancy in your life. Recognizing these signs is the first step in crafting a more harmonious composition for yourself.

- Patterns of Manipulation: This can appear as guilt-tripping, gaslighting (making you doubt your reality), or coercing you into decisions that don't align with your values. If you find yourself constantly second-guessing your feelings or actions due to someone else's influence, it's a red flag.
- Disrespectful Behavior: Healthy relationships thrive based on respect. Disrespect might manifest in belittling comments, ignoring your boundaries, or making you feel

inferior. A partner or friend who values you will treat you with kindness and consideration, even in disagreements.

- Lack of Support: Relationships should be your cheerleading squad, not a source of constant criticism or indifference. If you notice a pattern where your achievements are minimized or your struggles are dismissed, it might be time to reassess the health of the connection.

The impact of staying in toxic relationships can be profound, eroding the bedrock of self-love and confidence that you've built. It can leave you doubting your worth and questioning your ability to make healthy choices for yourself. Remember, the most important relationship you have is the one with yourself. Protecting this relationship means distancing yourself from negativity and those who do not have your best interests at heart.

Seeking support is crucial when untangling yourself from a toxic relationship. This can mean confiding in trusted friends or family members who can offer a supportive ear and helpful advice. In some cases, professional guidance from counselors or therapists can provide the tools and perspective needed to navigate away from unhealthy dynamics.

Moving forward after leaving a toxic relationship involves turning your attention inward, focusing on healing, and rebuilding the self-love that was compromised. Here are some steps to consider in this healing journey:

- Self-Care Practices: Reintroduce activities and practices that nurture your well-being. Toxic relationships can sometimes cause us to remove ourselves from activities that we enjoy. Start rediscovering those lost joys.

- Reflection: Spend time reflecting on the relationship and its impact on you. Journaling can be a therapeutic way to process your emotions and the lessons learned from the experience. This isn't about dwelling on the past but understanding it to make healthier choices in the future.
- Rebuilding Self-Esteem: Toxic relationships often chip away at your self-esteem. Rebuilding this crucial aspect of self-love might involve affirmations, therapy, and surrounding yourself with people who uplift you. Celebrate your strengths and accomplishments, no matter how small they seem.
- Setting Boundaries: Use this time to get clear on your boundaries—what you will and won't accept in relationships moving forward. Understanding and asserting your boundaries is a powerful way to protect your emotional well-being.
- Exploring New Interests: Sometimes, the end of a toxic relationship opens up space in your life for new opportunities. Explore new interests or revisit old ones. These can be sources of joy and pathways to meeting new people who share your values and interests.

Healing from a toxic relationship is not a linear process. There will be days of progress and perhaps moments of setbacks. What's important is that you keep moving forward, making choices that affirm your worth and contribute to your happiness. Remember, you deserve relationships that bring out the best in you, offering support, respect, and love in abundance. By recognizing the signs of toxicity, seeking support, and focusing on healing, you're taking important steps toward a happier, healthier future.

5.4 THE IMPORTANCE OF MUTUAL RESPECT

Mutual respect ensures relationships are not only strong but also enriching for everyone involved. Understanding mutual respect in relationships means recognizing each person's value ensuring their thoughts, feelings, and boundaries are acknowledged and honored. This concept is not just a nicety but a fundamental requirement for any healthy interaction, be it with friends, family, or romantic partners.

When we speak of mutual respect, we're talking about an environment where individuals feel safe to express themselves without fear of judgment or retaliation. It's a setting where differences are not just tolerated but appreciated, where open communication flourishes, and where individuals feel uplifted rather than diminished.

Respect and Self-Love

The journey to fostering mutual respect in any relationship starts within. It begins with how you treat yourself and how you respect your own needs, boundaries, and feelings. This self-respect sets the tone for what you expect from others and what you're willing to accept. It's a silent but powerful message about your worth. When you hold yourself in high regard, you naturally attract and gravitate toward people who mirror this respect back to you. Conversely, when you compromise on self-respect, you might find yourself in situations where your boundaries aren't honored, leading to relationships that feel draining rather than fulfilling.

The link between self-love and mutual respect is undeniable. Loving yourself involves recognizing your inherent worth, which in turn informs how you interact with others and what behaviors you're willing to accept. Self-love empowers you to assert your needs and encourages you to seek out relationships that are genuinely supportive and respectful.

Building Respectful Relationships

Creating and maintaining relationships grounded in mutual respect isn't an automatic process but a deliberate one. Here are some ways to ensure your relationships have a solid foundation of respect:

- Set Clear Boundaries: Clearly communicate your limits from the outset. Let people know what you're comfortable with and what crosses the line for you. This clarity helps prevent misunderstandings and ensures your interactions are respectful.
- Practice Active Listening: Show genuine interest in the other person's thoughts and feelings. Listen—not just to respond but to understand. This validates their feelings and shows that you value their perspective.
- Celebrate Differences: Embrace the differences between you and the other person as strengths rather than obstacles. Recognize that diverse opinions and experiences can enrich the relationship, offering new insights and growth opportunities.
- Reciprocate Respect: Respect is a two-way street. Make sure you're also treating the other person with the same level of respect you expect. Acknowledge their boundaries, listen attentively, and honor their feelings.

Dealing with Disrespect

Encountering disrespect within a relationship is a challenging but, unfortunately, not uncommon experience. Here's how to address and rectify situations where you feel disrespected:

- Identify the Behavior: Be clear about what actions or words felt disrespectful. Understanding exactly what bothered you is the first step in addressing the issue.
- Communicate Your Feelings: Approach the person and explain how their behavior affected you. Use "I" statements to express your feelings without placing blame, such as "I felt hurt when …"
- Seek to Understand: Sometimes, disrespect stems from misunderstandings or unawareness. Give the other person a chance to explain their side. This can lead to a deeper understanding and resolution.
- Reaffirm Boundaries: Remind the person of your boundaries. If the disrespect continues despite your efforts, it might be necessary to reevaluate the relationship and consider distancing yourself to protect your well-being.

Mutual respect is the cornerstone of any healthy relationship. It requires effort, communication, and, most importantly, a strong sense of self-worth. By cultivating self-love and self-respect, you set the stage for relationships that are enriching, supportive, and respectful. Remember, you deserve to be treated with kindness and consideration, and your relationships should reflect the love and respect you have for yourself.

5.5 FOSTERING EMPATHY AND UNDERSTANDING

Empathy, at its core, is about feeling with someone, not just for them. It's the bridge that connects us to the hearts of others, allowing us to see the world through their eyes, feel what they feel, and understand their perspectives. This ability to tune into another's emotional world is what strengthens the bonds we share, making empathy a crucial element in building and maintaining healthy relationships.

Empathy as a Relationship Builder

Empathy binds people together through shared experiences and emotions. When you empathize with someone, you're acknowledging their feelings as valid and important. This recognition can significantly deepen the sense of trust and closeness in a relationship. It tells the other person, "You're not alone," fostering a sense of safety and belonging that encourages open and honest communication.

Practicing Empathy

Empathy might seem like an innate trait, but it's also a skill that can be developed and refined with practice. Here are some ways to cultivate empathy in your daily interactions:

- Active Listening: Give your full attention to the person speaking. Avoid the impulse to formulate your response while they're still talking. Instead, focus on understanding their message and the emotions behind it.
- Perspective-Taking: Try to put yourself in the other person's shoes, imagining how you would feel if you were

in their situation. This can help you grasp the emotional depth of what they're experiencing.

- Validation: Acknowledge the other person's feelings without trying to fix them. Sometimes, people just need to feel heard and understood, not necessarily advised or corrected.
- Expressing Empathy: Use phrases like "That sounds really tough" or "I can imagine how that must feel" to convey empathy. These expressions show you're trying to connect with their emotional experience.

Overcoming Empathy Blocks

While the path to empathy can be rewarding, it's not without its obstacles. Prejudices, biases, and personal judgments can cloud our ability to empathize with others. Recognizing these blocks is the first step in overcoming them:

- Awareness: Pay attention to the moments when you find it hard to empathize. Ask yourself if there are preconceived notions or biases influencing your reaction.
- Curiosity: Approach situations with an open mind and a willingness to learn about the other person's experiences. This can help dismantle stereotypes or judgments that block empathy.
- Practice Compassion: Extend kindness to yourself when you notice these blocks. Remember, recognizing and working through biases is a part of growth.

Empathy and Self-Love

The relationship between self-love and empathy is a dynamic interplay where nurturing one can enhance the other. Loving yourself fosters a deeper understanding of your own emotions, which, in turn, can make it easier to connect with the emotions of others. When you're compassionate toward yourself, you're more likely to extend that compassion to those around you. Thus, the journey of self-love not only enriches your inner world but also empowers you to engage more empathetically in your relationships.

As we wrap up our exploration of empathy and its role in cultivating understanding and connection, we're reminded of the profound impact it has on our relationships. From actively listening and taking the perspective of others to expressing empathy and working through our biases, these practices enable us to build stronger, more meaningful connections. Empathy not only bridges gaps between people but also enriches our own emotional lives, creating a cycle of mutual understanding and support.

Looking ahead, the skills and insights we've gained here lay the groundwork for navigating the complexities of relationships with grace and empathy. As we move forward, we carry with us the knowledge that empathy, rooted in self-love, is a cornerstone of healthy, fulfilling relationships.

NURTURING FAMILY BONDS WITH SELF-LOVE

Your family can be likened to a team working together to build a beautiful, sturdy house. Each member has their own role, from laying bricks to painting walls. Just like in building a home and nurturing family relationships, every action you take and every word you speak contributes to the strength and beauty of the family unit. At the heart of this collaborative effort is self-love—like the blueprint guiding the construction, ensuring that every room radiates warmth and every corner is filled with light.

6.1 GROWING TOGETHER: SELF-LOVE AND FAMILY DYNAMICS

Self-Love in the Family Context

Self-love within a family acts much like the roots of a tree, providing stability and nourishment. When each family member acknowledges their own worth, understands their needs, and treats themselves with kindness, it sets a tone of respect and care throughout the household. It's a reminder that everyone deserves love and understanding, starting from within. This mutual recognition can significantly reduce conflicts, as each person feels valued and understood.

Practical Tip: Hold a family meeting where each person shares something they appreciate about themselves. It could be a talent, a trait, or an accomplishment. This practice not only boosts individual self-esteem but also encourages a culture of appreciation and respect.

Supporting Family Members

Supporting each other's journeys toward self-love means being there for the highs and the lows. It's about celebrating successes without jealousy and offering comfort during hard times without judgment. This support creates a safety net, reassuring every family member that they're not alone, no matter what.

When and How: Make it a habit to check in with each other regularly. During dinner, for instance, you could have a round-table discussion where everyone shares the best and most challenging parts of their day.

Shared Activities for Bonding

Shared activities are the threads that weave the fabric of family life tighter. These can range from preparing a meal together to going on a hike or even tackling a DIY project as a team. Activities like these not only create cherished memories but also opportunities for open communication and mutual support, reinforcing the bonds of love and understanding.

Activity Idea: Plan a monthly "family adventure day." Let a different member choose the activity each time. Whether it's visiting a museum, hiking, or a movie marathon at home, the key is doing something enjoyable together, fostering a sense of unity and shared joy.

Handling Family Conflict

Conflicts, while challenging, are a natural part of family life. They're not roadblocks but rather signposts, pointing to areas where growth and understanding can occur. Approaching conflicts with empathy, open-mindedness, and a willingness to listen can transform these moments into opportunities for strengthening relationships.

Conflict Resolution Strategy: Next time a conflict arises, try the "pause and reflect" method before responding. Take a deep breath, consider the other person's perspective, and then express your feelings calmly and clearly. It's about responding, not reacting.

Nurturing family bonds with self-love is hard work. It requires patience, effort, and the right conditions to flourish. But the result —a family where each member feels seen, valued, and supported— is undoubtedly worth it. Through practices that promote self-love, shared activities that strengthen connections, and compassionate approaches to conflict, families can grow together, building a home where everyone thrives.

6.2 HEALTHY COMMUNICATION WITH FAMILY MEMBERS

In the mosaic of family life, each piece—each person—contributes to the overall picture. How we communicate can either enhance the beauty of this picture or detract from it. Let's explore ways to ensure our family interactions add vibrancy and depth to our collective lives.

Communicating Needs and Boundaries

Clear communication is like the sunlight that nourishes the garden of our family relationships, allowing them to bloom. Expressing needs and setting boundaries is akin to tending to this garden with care, ensuring every plant gets its share of light and space to grow.

- Start by understanding your own needs and boundaries. Reflect on what matters most to you in your family interactions. Is it respect for personal space, uninterrupted time to pursue hobbies, or perhaps more open discussions about emotions?
- Approach the conversation with love and respect, focusing on how fulfilling these needs will benefit not just you but the family as a whole. For instance, explain how having a quiet hour for reading in the evening will make you more present and engaged during family time.
- Use specific examples and avoid vague statements. Instead of saying, "I need more space," you might say, "I would appreciate having some time alone in my room after dinner to unwind."
- Remember, it's about finding a balance that honors everyone's needs. Be open to compromise and discussion.

Active Listening in the Family

Active listening is the water that sustains the garden, keeping the soil moist and receptive. When we truly listen to our family members, we're not just hearing their words; we're understanding their emotions, perspectives, and underlying needs.

- Give your full attention. This means putting aside distractions like phones or other tasks and focusing entirely on the person speaking.
- Show that you're listening. Nod in agreement, make eye contact, and use verbal affirmations like "I see" or "That makes sense."
- Reflect back on what you've heard to ensure you've understood correctly. For example, "So what you're saying is that you feel overwhelmed with work?"
- Ask open-ended questions to encourage deeper sharing. Questions like "How did that make you feel?" or "What would help you in this situation?" can open doors to more meaningful conversations.

Navigating Difficult Conversations

Difficult conversations test our resilience within our family. Yet, they're necessary for growth. Approaching these talks with empathy, patience, and openness can turn potential conflicts into opportunities for strengthening bonds.

- Choose the right time and place. Ensure that you won't be interrupted and that everyone is in a calm state of mind. Sometimes, setting an agreed-upon time to talk can help all parties prepare emotionally and mentally.
- Start with positive affirmations or shared goals to set a cooperative tone. You might say, "I know we both want what's best for me, so let's try to figure this out together."
- Use "I" statements to express your feelings without placing blame. Replace "You never help with household chores" with "I feel overwhelmed when I have to do the chores on my own."

- Stay focused on the issue at hand. Avoid bringing up past grievances or unrelated topics, which can derail the conversation.

The Role of Apologies

A sincere apology acknowledges mistakes, shows empathy for the hurt caused, and commits to doing better. It's a powerful tool for mending fences and revitalizing our connections.

- Acknowledge the specific actions or words that caused hurt. General apologies can feel insincere or dismissive.
- Express genuine remorse. Let them know you understand the impact of your actions and that you truly regret the hurt caused.
- Make amends or change behavior. Apologies are only as strong as the actions that follow them. Show through your actions that you're committed to making things right.
- Don't expect immediate forgiveness. Give the other person time to process and heal. Patience and continued respect for their feelings are key.

6.3 SETTING BOUNDARIES AT HOME

At home, setting boundaries is not about building walls between us but rather drawing lines in the sand that help everyone understand where they stand and how they can best support each other. It's about creating a space where individuality is respected, personal growth is encouraged, and mutual respect flourishes.

Importance of Boundaries

Boundaries within a family context serve as the foundation for a healthy, supportive environment. They help us define what we are comfortable with, how we wish to be treated, and how we interact with one another. By establishing these limits, we not only protect our well-being but also promote an atmosphere of mutual respect. This clarity reduces misunderstandings and conflicts, making it easier for everyone to navigate their relationships with confidence and care.

Examples of Healthy Boundaries

- Personal Space: This can range from having a private space where family members can retreat when they need time alone to set limits on how personal items are shared or borrowed.
- Privacy: Respecting privacy involves knocking before entering someone's room, not reading someone else's messages or journals without permission, and understanding that everyone has the right to keep certain thoughts or feelings to themselves if they choose.
- Emotional Limits: Recognizing that everyone has different emotional capacities and triggers. It's important to refrain from forcing someone to engage in conversations or activities that make them uncomfortable and to respect their need to process emotions at their own pace.

Setting boundaries around time can also be crucial, such as respecting study, work, or relaxation times without unnecessary interruptions.

Communicating Boundaries to Family

Effectively conveying your boundaries to family members requires clarity, empathy, and a dose of courage. Here's how to approach it:

- Clarity and Specificity: Be clear and specific about what your boundaries are. Rather than saying, "I need space," say, "I would like to have an hour of alone time after dinner to relax and recharge."
- Focus on Feelings: Explain how it makes you feel when your boundaries are not respected. This can help others understand the importance of these boundaries to your well-being.
- Positive Framing: Frame your boundaries in a positive light. Instead of focusing on what others shouldn't do, highlight how respecting these boundaries will improve family harmony and individual happiness.
- Offer Reassurance: Reassure your family members that setting boundaries is not about creating distance but about fostering healthier, more respectful relationships.

For younger family members or those not accustomed to discussing boundaries, using examples or role-playing scenarios can help illustrate the concept more vividly.

Respecting Others' Boundaries

Just as we wish our boundaries to be respected, it's vital to extend the same courtesy to other family members. Here are ways to cultivate a culture of respect at home:

- Active Listening: When a family member communicates their boundaries, listen actively. Show that you understand and respect their needs by acknowledging and adjusting your behavior accordingly.
- Ask, Don't Assume: If you're unsure whether something falls within someone's comfort zone, ask. It's better to have a conversation than to unintentionally overstep.
- Model Respectful Behavior: Demonstrate through your actions how to respect others' boundaries. This can be particularly impactful in families with children, as it sets a positive example for them to follow.
- Encourage Open Dialogue: Foster an environment where family members feel comfortable discussing and renegotiating boundaries as needed. People grow and change, and so, too, may their boundaries.

In the dance of family life, boundaries are not constraints but rather the steps that allow everyone to move together in harmony. They enable us to interact with love and respect, understanding and celebrating our differences while supporting our collective well-being. By setting, communicating, and respecting boundaries at home, we weave a stronger, more vibrant family life where each member feels valued and understood.

6.4 THE ROLE OF FORGIVENESS IN STRENGTHENING BONDS

Forgiveness within the family setting can sometimes feel like a complicated dance, one where steps are missed and toes occasionally get stepped on. Yet, this dance of forgiveness, when performed with understanding and genuine intent, can lead to a more harmonious and connected family life. It's about moving beyond past hurts and misunderstandings to a place of mutual respect and love.

Understanding Forgiveness

Forgiveness is the act of letting go of resentment, anger, or the desire for retribution against a family member who has caused you pain or wrongdoing. It's not about condoning the behavior or forgetting it happened, but rather choosing to release the grip that past hurts have on your present interactions. The benefits of this practice are manifold, leading to reduced stress, improved mental health, and stronger, more resilient relationships. However, the path to forgiveness can be fraught with challenges, as it often requires confronting painful emotions and overcoming pride or stubbornness.

- Recognizing the Wrong: Before forgiveness can truly begin, there must be an acknowledgment of the hurtful action or words. This step is crucial for both the person seeking forgiveness and the one offering it.
- Empathy and Understanding: Trying to see the situation from the other person's perspective is a key part of the forgiveness process. It can help in understanding their motivations and the circumstances that led to their actions.

Forgiveness and Self-Love

At its heart, forgiveness is deeply tied to self-love. Holding onto anger and resentment can be like carrying a heavy burden that weighs down your spirit and clouds your ability to experience joy and peace. By choosing to forgive, you're not only offering a gift to the person who wronged you but also to yourself. It's a declaration that you value your well-being and peace of mind above holding onto past grievances. This act of self-care can significantly enhance your emotional and mental health, paving the way for more loving and positive interactions within your family.

- Release Negative Emotions: Forgiveness allows you to let go of negative emotions that can be harmful to your well-being. It's a step toward healing and finding peace.
- Reconnect with Your Values: Forgiving someone aligns with the values of compassion, empathy, and understanding, reinforcing your commitment to living according to these principles.

Steps to Forgiveness

Forgiving a family member is a process that can vary greatly from one person to another. However, certain steps can guide you along the way:

- Reflect on the Situation: Take some time to think about the incident and how it has affected you. This can help you understand why forgiveness feels challenging and what emotions are tied to the event.
- Express Your Feelings: Find a safe space to share your feelings about what happened. This could be through a conversation with the person involved, writing a letter (even if you never send it), or discussing it with a trusted friend or therapist.
- Decide to Forgive: Forgiveness is a choice. It's a decision you make to move forward. This doesn't happen overnight and may require you to reaffirm your choice daily until it feels more natural.
- Let Go of Resentment: This is perhaps the most challenging step, as it involves consciously choosing to release feelings of bitterness or anger. It might help to

remind yourself why you're choosing forgiveness and the benefits it will bring to your life.

Rebuilding Trust

After forgiveness, the next step in healing family relationships is rebuilding trust. This process takes time and effort from all parties involved and is built on a foundation of open communication, consistent behavior, and patience.

- Start Small: Trust is rebuilt through small, consistent actions over time. Start with low-stakes situations to gradually restore confidence in the reliability and sincerity of the family member.
- Open Communication: Keep the lines of communication open. Discuss what actions or behaviors are needed to rebuild trust and be open about your feelings during the process.
- Show Patience: Understand that rebuilding trust doesn't happen overnight. There will be setbacks along the way, but with patience and persistence, progress can be made.
- Consistent Efforts: Consistency is key to rebuilding trust. Make a concerted effort to follow through on promises and demonstrate through your actions that you are committed to mending the relationship.

In navigating the waters of forgiveness and rebuilding trust within the family, remember that these processes are not linear. They ebb and flow, with progress and setbacks along the way. Yet, the effort to forgive and rebuild trust is a powerful testament to the strength and resilience of family bonds. It's about choosing love, understanding, and peace, creating a family dynamic that is supportive, respectful, and deeply connected.

6.5 CELEBRATING FAMILY MILESTONES WITH LOVE

Every part of family life is composed of moments of triumph, learning, and growth. Celebrating these milestones enriches your family story with layers of joy, achievement, and mutual support. It's through these celebrations that families not only recognize individual and collective accomplishments but also reinforce the bonds that unite them.

Importance of Celebration

Acknowledging milestones and achievements within the family serves a dual purpose. Firstly, it acts as an affirmation of the hard work, dedication, and perseverance that went into reaching a particular goal. Whether it's a graduation, a new job, mastering a new skill, or even overcoming a personal challenge, celebrating these moments highlights their significance. Secondly, it nurtures a culture of support and encouragement. By celebrating together, families send a clear message: "We see you, we're proud of you, and your achievements matter to us."

To truly honor these milestones, consider:

- Creating a "celebration jar" where family members can drop notes about small wins or things they're grateful for throughout the week. Dedicate time during family gatherings to read these notes aloud.
- Encouraging each family member to share their achievements, no matter how big or small, fosters an environment where everyone's accomplishments are valued.

Planning Meaningful Celebrations

The essence of a meaningful celebration lies not in its grandeur or extravagance but in its ability to reflect the personality and preferences of the honoree. Tailoring celebrations to the individual or the family as a whole adds a layer of personal significance to the event.

Here are some ideas for planning celebrations that truly resonate:

- For academic achievements, instead of the traditional dinner out, perhaps the honoree would enjoy a day dedicated to their favorite hobby, be it hiking, painting, or visiting a museum.
- Celebrating personal growth milestones, such as overcoming a fear or developing a new skill, with a custom-made gift that symbolizes achievement. A piece of jewelry, a book, or a handmade item can serve as a lasting reminder of their journey.

Creating Traditions of Love

Family traditions are the rituals that give rhythm to our lives. They're the repeated acts that, over time, instill a unity of shared history and identity. Creating traditions centered around celebration and love reinforces a sense of belonging and reinforces the family's values of support and acknowledgment.

- Annual family photo shoots to commemorate another year of growth and change. These photos serve as visual milestones, capturing the evolution of the family over time.

- A "day of yes" tradition, where the person being celebrated gets to make all the decisions for the day, from what to eat to what activities to do. This tradition can make the honoree feel special and valued.

Reflecting on Growth Together

Taking the time to reflect as a family on the journey leading to each milestone fosters a deeper appreciation for the challenges overcome and the lessons learned. It's a practice that not only honors the individual's growth but also highlights the supportive role the family has played in that journey.

- Hold a reflection session as part of the celebration, where family members can share how they've seen the honoree grow, recount memories related to the milestone, and express their hopes for the future.
- Create a "milestone memory book" where reflections, photos, and notes about each major family milestone are kept. Over time, this book becomes a precious record of the family's journey, filled with stories of resilience, growth, and love.

By making celebrations a consistent part of family life, we do more than mark achievements; we create a culture of love, support, and mutual respect. These celebrations are reminders of the strength that lies in unity, the joy in shared success, and the beauty of moving forward together. As we turn the page, let's carry with us the understanding that the way we honor our milestones can profoundly shape the spirit of our family, fostering connections that endure and inspire.

As this chapter draws to a close, we're reminded of the power held in moments of celebration. These are the times when the essence of family—its love, resilience, and unity—is most vividly expressed. Through planning meaningful celebrations, creating traditions of love, and reflecting on our journey together, we strengthen the ties that bind us, ensuring that every achievement, big or small, is a step forward for the family as a whole. Looking ahead, let's continue to nurture these bonds, allowing them to guide us through life's many chapters with grace and love.

GOAL SETTING – CRAFTING YOUR PATH WITH SELF-LOVE

Imagine standing at the base of a vast mountain range. Before you stretch countless peaks, each representing a dream or aspiration you hold dear. Some peaks might seem impossibly high, while others are more accessible, yet each calls to you, inviting you to embark on an adventure. In this metaphor, self-love is your compass and map, guiding and encouraging you as you navigate this terrain. It's about recognizing that while the journey to each summit might be challenging, the path you carve out—steeped in self-respect and kindness toward yourself—makes the adventure worthwhile.

In real life, our goals can sometimes feel as daunting as towering mountains. Yet, when we ground our goal setting in self-love, we approach these challenges with a sense of compassion and encouragement for ourselves, transforming the journey into one of discovery and fulfillment.

7.1 DREAMING BIG: THE ROLE OF SELF-LOVE IN GOAL SETTING

Self-Love as Motivation

Self-love motivates us by ensuring our goals genuinely reflect who we are and what we value rather than what we think we should aim for based on external pressures or expectations. It's like choosing a mountain to climb because it calls to your heart, not because someone else told you it's the one you should conquer.

- Real-life example: I always knew I wanted to pursue a career in engineering, but my family and friends wanted me to go into the family business or a field that they were interested in. I ended up staying true to myself and going to school for an engineering career. If you're passionate about something like art but feel pressured to pursue a more "practical" career, self-love encourages you to consider goals that align with your true interests, such as taking art classes or setting up an online portfolio.

Aligning Goals with Values

Aligning your goals with your values can help guide you through difficult or uncertain times. It ensures that every step forward is a step toward a life that feels meaningful and fulfilling to you. Consider the following questions when thinking about and building your goals:

- What values are most important to me? (E.g., creativity, helping others, independence.)
- Do my current goals reflect these values?
- How can I adjust my goals to better align with my values?

Setting Achievable Milestones

Breaking down your larger goals into smaller, achievable milestones makes the journey feel less daunting and more manageable. It's like plotting a route up the mountain that includes camps along the way, allowing you to rest and celebrate your progress. Follow the below example to see how you can start filling out your own Goal-Setting Worksheet:

Goal-Setting Worksheet Example

- Goal: *Learn to play the guitar and perform a song at a local open mic night.*
- Milestones:

  - *Acquire a beginner's guitar and basic learning materials.*
  - *Master three basic chords (e.g., C, G, and D) and practice smooth chord transitions.*
  - *Learn to play a chosen song from start to finish.*

- Deadline for each milestone:

  - *Obtain guitar and learning materials—within the **first two weeks**.*
  - *Master three basic chords and transitions—within the **first month**.*
  - *Learn to play the chosen song—within **two to three months**.*

Celebrating Progress

Celebrating each step of progress reinforces self-love and motivates you to continue. Acknowledge every milestone as a victory in its own right. This can be as simple as treating yourself to your favorite snack or as significant as a day off just for yourself.

> **Real-life example**: I played basketball in high school, and I knew I wanted to be captain of the team. I practiced hard and went to training camps to be the best I could be. I worked hard and earned my spot on the team as captain. Following a successful season, I took the time to celebrate with my family and mark the achieved goal. I was able to rest and reflect on all of the efforts I made to achieve something great. It was only after this time of rest and reflection that I began to chart my course for my next goal.

In the grand scheme, setting goals from a place of self-love means embracing your aspirations with open arms and recognizing the courage it takes to chase after what truly lights up your soul. It's about plotting a course that's uniquely yours, one that honors your values, celebrates your progress, and respects your well-being every step of the way. Through this approach, goal setting transforms from a daunting task into an exciting journey of self-discovery and fulfillment.

7.2 BREAKING GOALS INTO ACHIEVABLE STEPS

Setting goals is akin to sketching a map for an adventure—it outlines the path, but the journey itself is filled with discoveries, challenges, and victories. The method of breaking goals into achievable steps ensures that each part of the journey is marked by progress, no matter how incremental it may seem. This approach not only makes your aspirations more tangible but also infuses your path with a sense of clarity and purpose.

SMART Goals

The concept of SMART goals pushes us toward setting objectives that are not just dreams but achievable realities. SMART stands for Specific, Measurable, Achievable, Relevant, and Time-Bound, each a critical ingredient in the recipe for successful goal setting:

- Specific: Define your goal with as much detail as possible. Knowing precisely what you aim to achieve gives your efforts direction.
- Measurable: Establish concrete criteria for tracking progress. Seeing how far you've come keeps motivation high.
- Achievable: Ensure the goal is within your reach. While it's good to aim high, unrealistic goals can lead to discouragement.
- Relevant: Align your goal with your broader aspirations. This ensures that every achievement brings you closer to your ultimate vision.
- Time-Bound: Set a deadline. A sense of urgency can spur action and prevent procrastination.

Applying SMART criteria transforms vague wishes into clear, actionable objectives, each step a milestone in the adventure of realizing your dreams.

Overcoming Overwhelm

Encountering a sense of overwhelm is not uncommon on this path. The key is to navigate through this feeling with strategies that bring focus and perspective:

- List Making: Start by writing down every task, no matter how big or small. This act alone can reduce anxiety by making your goals seem more manageable.
- Break Tasks Down: Divide larger tasks into smaller, more manageable parts. This can make even the most daunting task seem achievable.
- Prioritize: Identify tasks that are urgent and important. Tackling these first can relieve pressure and create momentum.
- One Step at a Time: Focus on one task at a time. Trying to juggle multiple tasks simultaneously can dilute your efforts and lead to burnout.

By adopting these strategies, you can clear the fog of overwhelm, allowing your direction and focus to emerge with renewed clarity.

Adapting Goals

As you move forward, you'll find that growth and change are constants on this journey. Your goals, too, need to reflect this fluidity, adapting as you gain new insights and experiences:

- Regular Reviews: Set aside time to review your goals regularly. This helps identify what's working, what isn't, and what has changed in your aspirations or circumstances.

- Stay Open: Embrace the idea that it's okay to modify your goals. Rigidity can hinder progress, while flexibility opens up new possibilities.
- Celebrate Learning: Each attempt, successful or not, is packed with lessons. Viewing changes in plans as opportunities for growth can transform setbacks into stepping stones.

This adaptable approach ensures that your goals remain aligned with your evolving self, making each step forward meaningful and enriched with personal growth.

Visualizing Success

The practice of visualizing success acts as a powerful motivator, painting a vivid picture of your achievements even before they materialize. This technique involves:

- Creating a Clear Image: Close your eyes and imagine achieving your goal in as much detail as possible. What does it look like? How do you feel?
- Use All Senses: Incorporate all your senses into this visualization. The more real it feels, the more potent its impact on your motivation and confidence.
- Positive Reinforcement: Pair visualization with positive affirmations. This reinforces the belief in your ability to succeed and navigates your subconscious toward making your vision a reality.
- Regular Practice: Make visualization a regular part of your routine. Before starting your day, spend a few moments envisioning your success. This sets a positive tone and sharpens your focus on your objectives.

By vividly picturing your success, you're not just dreaming about the future; you're actively pulling it toward your present, fueling your journey with inspiration and drive.

As you embark on this adventure of breaking goals into achievable steps, remember each step taken is a victory in itself. Through SMART planning, navigating overwhelm with grace, adapting with flexibility, and visualizing success, you're not just moving toward your goals; you're weaving a journey rich with learning, growth, and fulfillment.

7.3 OVERCOMING SETBACKS WITH SELF-COMPASSION

Setbacks are akin to missteps in a dance. They're inevitable, yet they don't define the performance; it's how we recover that shapes our path forward. The art of navigating these moments with self-compassion is like learning a choreography that respects our rhythm, allowing us to move through disappointments with understanding and kindness toward ourselves.

Expecting and Accepting Setbacks

It's natural to envision a smooth ascent toward our goals, but reality often presents a series of ups and downs. Accepting that setbacks are part of the process is crucial. They're not signs of failure but markers of effort and growth. When you start with the understanding that challenges are part of the landscape, you're better prepared to face them with resilience.

- Normalize the experience by reminding yourself that everyone encounters setbacks. It's not a reflection of your worth or capability.

- Adopt a mindset that views these moments as expected turns in the road, not roadblocks. This shift in perspective can reduce the impact of disappointment and foster a more compassionate approach to self-evaluation.

Learning from Failure

Reframing failure as a learning opportunity is transformative. It allows us to extract valuable insights from our experiences, turning what might initially feel like a setback into a stepping stone. Each time something doesn't go as planned, it's an invitation to pause, reflect, and gather wisdom for the next attempt.

- After a setback, ask yourself, "What can I learn from this?" Whether it's a realization about your methods, a need for additional resources, or insights into your resilience, every failure has something to teach.
- Document these lessons. Creating a record of what didn't work and how you plan to adjust your approach can be a powerful tool for growth. It's a tangible reminder of your evolving strategy and resilience.

Self-Talk during Challenges

The words we speak to ourselves in moments of difficulty have profound power. They can either lift us up or weigh us down. Cultivating positive self-talk is like composing a supportive inner narrative that encourages us to persevere.

- Be mindful of the language you use with yourself. Replace critical or negative self-statements with kinder, more constructive messages. For instance, instead of saying, "I always mess up," try, "I'm learning, and I'll do better next time."

- Practice affirmations that reinforce your strength and ability to overcome challenges. Phrases like "I am resilient" or "I grow with every experience" can be powerful motivators.

Seeking Support

While the journey toward our goals is personal, we don't have to walk it alone. Reaching out for support from friends, family, or mentors can provide a sense of solidarity and perspective. It's a reminder that help is available and that sharing our struggles can lighten the load.

- Identify people in your life who offer constructive feedback and encouragement. Let them know when you're facing a tough time, and be open to their insights and support.
- Consider joining groups or communities with similar goals. These spaces can offer invaluable motivation, advice, and companionship. They remind us that setbacks are universal and surmountable.

In navigating the path of goal achievement, setbacks are not detours but integral parts of the journey. They test our resolve, teach us invaluable lessons, and ultimately make our successes even sweeter. By approaching these moments with self-compassion, learning from each experience, engaging in positive self-talk, and seeking support when needed, we equip ourselves with the tools to continue forward with resilience and grace.

7.4 THE IMPORTANCE OF PERSISTENCE AND PATIENCE

The virtues of persistence and patience often stand as unsung heroes when it comes to achieving our goals. While the glow of triumph might be the end goal, the true magic happens in the spaces between, where determination and a steady pace turn dreams into reality. This section unfolds the layers of these virtues, offering insights into their pivotal role and practical ways to weave them into our aspirations.

The Power of Persistence

Imagine facing a steep hill during a marathon. Each step feels heavier than the last, your breath is short, and the summit seems just out of reach. In this moment, the essence of persistence shines brightest. It's the inner resolve that whispers, "Keep going, one step at a time," turning the seemingly insurmountable into the achievable.

Persistence is not merely about stubbornness or blind determination; it's a nuanced dance with our goals, marked by an understanding that setbacks are not the end but part of the process. Here's how to cultivate it:

- Break It Down: When a goal feels overwhelming, dissect it into smaller, more manageable tasks. Achieving these smaller victories fuels your drive to continue.
- Remind Yourself Why: On days when motivation wanes, remind yourself why you set this goal. A visual representation, like a vision board or a written statement, can serve as a powerful reminder.

- Stay Flexible: Be open to adjusting your strategies if something isn't working. Flexibility allows you to navigate obstacles without losing sight of your ultimate goal.

Cultivating Patience

Patience in the pursuit of goals is like nurturing a seedling. It demands faith in the unseen, knowing that, with time and care, growth is happening beneath the surface. It teaches us to value the present moment and understand that some things cannot be rushed.

Here are techniques to foster patience:

- Mindfulness Practices: Engaging in mindfulness or meditation can enhance your ability to stay present and reduce the rush toward immediate results. It helps to appreciate the present while working toward the future.
- Track Your Progress: Keep a log of your progress. Seeing how far you've come can be a source of encouragement on days when patience wears thin.
- Set Realistic Expectations: Understanding that meaningful achievements take time can help temper impatience. Remind yourself that quick results are not always lasting results.

Balancing Ambition with Self-Care

While ambition drives us forward, ensuring we don't lose ourselves in the pursuit is crucial. The balance between striving for our goals and maintaining our well-being is delicate but essential. Ignoring self-care in the name of ambition can lead to burnout, where both our goals and our health suffer.

To maintain this balance:

- Schedule Downtime: Integrate regular breaks and leisure activities into your schedule. This downtime is not wasted time but an investment in your long-term productivity and creativity.
- Listen to Your Body: Pay attention to signs of stress or fatigue. Your body's signals are a guide to when you need to slow down and replenish your energy.
- Seek Joy in the Process: Find aspects of your goal pursuit that bring you joy. This could be the learning involved, the people you meet, or the small successes along the way.

Embracing the Journey

Focusing solely on the destination can make the path there seem laborious and full of trials. However, when we shift our perspective to embrace the journey itself, we open ourselves up to a world of discovery and personal growth. This mindset allows us to find fulfillment not just in achieving our goals but in the rich experiences gathered along the way.

To embrace the journey, consider:

- Celebrate Learning: Every challenge faced and obstacle overcome is a lesson learned. Celebrate these as integral parts of your growth.
- Find Meaning in the Moments: Look for the value in each step of your journey. Whether it's a skill acquired, a connection made, or a new insight, these moments are the milestones of your personal evolution.

- Adjust Your Pace: Remember that rushing can lead to missed opportunities for growth. Adjust your pace to one that allows you to savor the experiences and lessons along the way.

In weaving persistence and patience into the pursuit of our goals, we allow ourselves the space to grow, learn, and ultimately achieve with a sense of completeness and well-being. These virtues remind us that the path to our dreams is as rich and rewarding as the dreams themselves, inviting us to move forward with a heart full of determination and a pace guided by wisdom.

7.5 CELEBRATING YOUR ACHIEVEMENTS

When you reach a milestone, taking the time to honor your hard work and dedication is more than a mere act of celebration—it's a vital component of your growth and journey toward self-love. This moment of pause allows you to soak in the reality of your accomplishment, reminding you of your capability and resilience.

Recognizing Your Successes

Acknowledging your achievements, big or small, plays a crucial role in building your self-confidence and motivating you for future endeavors. It's easy to brush past these moments, rushing toward the next goal without stopping to reflect on what you've accomplished. However, every success, no matter its size, is a testament to your effort and determination. Creating a ritual around celebrating these successes can reinforce their significance. This could be as simple as writing down what you've achieved in a dedicated notebook or as elaborate as organizing a small gathering with close friends or family to share in your joy.

Sharing Your Achievements

Opening up about your successes with others not only multiplies your joy but also creates a sense of community and shared happiness. It invites those around you to partake in your achievement, offering support and acknowledgment that can further bolster your sense of accomplishment. Moreover, sharing your journey can inspire others to pursue their goals, creating a ripple effect of motivation and encouragement within your circle. Next time you achieve something, big or small, share it with a friend family member, or even on social media. It's a way to extend the joy and potentially inspire someone else on their path.

Reflecting on the Journey

While reaching a goal is indeed a cause for celebration, the true value often lies in the journey itself—the challenges you've overcome, the knowledge you've gained, and the person you've become in the process. Dedicating time to reflect on these aspects allows you to appreciate the depth of your achievement and the growth that has occurred along the way. This reflection can take many forms, from a quiet moment of contemplation to writing a detailed account of your journey in a journal.

> **Reflection prompts**: What obstacles did I encounter, and how did I overcome them? What have I learned about myself through this process? How has this achievement changed me?

Setting New Goals

With each achievement celebrated and reflected upon, the horizon of possibility expands, inviting you to set new goals. This cycle of setting, pursuing, and celebrating goals is not just about achieving external markers of success; it's about continuous growth, self-discovery, and pushing the boundaries of what you thought possible. As you contemplate your next objective, consider how your recent achievement has shaped your aspirations and what new challenges you're now equipped to tackle.

> **Future aspirations**: Consider how your recent success influences your future goals. What new opportunities have opened up? How have your interests or priorities shifted?

By taking the time to celebrate your achievements, share your successes, reflect on your journey, and set new goals, you're not just marking milestones; you're pouring into your book of experiences that tell the story of who you are and who you're becoming. This process, rooted in self-love and acknowledgment, is a powerful force for personal transformation, driving you forward with a sense of purpose and fulfillment.

Let this be a reminder to honor every step you take, every hurdle you overcome, and every milestone you reach. These moments are the building blocks of your story, contributing to a larger narrative of growth, resilience, and the unwavering pursuit of what brings you joy and fulfillment. As we move forward, carry with you the lessons learned, the joy of each accomplishment, and the excitement for the adventures that lie ahead.

EMBRACING YOUR ROLE IN THE WORLD

In this chapter, we dive into the empowering act of advocacy, the courage it takes to stand up for what you believe in, and the invaluable support of a community that amplifies your voice. It's about making your mark in a way that's true to you, all while navigating the challenges and resistance that might come your way.

8.1 FINDING YOUR VOICE: ADVOCACY AND SELF-LOVE

Self-Love and Self-Expression

Self-love does more than just fuel your sense of worth; it's the backbone of your voice in this world. When you value yourself, you understand the importance of your thoughts, feelings, and beliefs. It empowers you to express them and stand up for what you believe in. Think of it this way: if self-love is knowing your song by heart, self-expression is singing it out loud, regardless of who's listening.

It's like choosing to wear your favorite outfit, not because it's trendy, but because it makes you feel good. That act of choosing what makes you happy, despite any fashion norms, is a form of self-expression rooted in self-love.

Advocacy as Empowerment

Standing up for causes that resonate with you is a powerful form of self-love. It's acknowledging that your voice matters and can be a force for change. Whether it's volunteering for an environmental campaign or speaking out on social issues, advocacy is about aligning your actions with your values. It's the realization that you have the power to make a difference, not just in your life but in the lives of others, too.

When you advocate for something you believe in, you're saying, "This is important to me." It's like when you recommend your favorite book to a friend because you believe they'll benefit from it, too. That recommendation is an act of advocacy on a small scale.

Navigating Resistance

Facing criticism or pushback is a common part of advocacy. Not everyone will agree with you, and that's okay. What's important is staying true to your beliefs, even when it's tough. Here are some strategies for dealing with resistance:

- Stay Informed: Know your facts. The more knowledgeable you are about your cause, the more confidently you can speak about it.

- Seek Support: Surround yourself with people who share your values and can offer encouragement when things get tough.
- Remember Your Why: When faced with resistance, remind yourself why you're advocating for this cause. It can help keep your spirits up.

Building a Supportive Community

Finding or creating a community of like-minded individuals can amplify your advocacy efforts and provide a network of support. It's like joining a book club because you love reading. In a book club, members support each other's love for literature, discuss different views, and celebrate shared interests. Similarly, being part of a community that cares about the same issues as you do can make your advocacy journey less lonely and more impactful.

- Start Small: Look for local groups or online forums dedicated to your cause. Attending meetings or participating in discussions can be a good starting point.
- Be Active: Don't just join a group; be an active member. Share your ideas, volunteer for activities, and contribute to the community.
- Create Your Own: If you can't find a community that fits, consider starting your own. Social media platforms can be a great place to connect with others who share your interests.

In this chapter, we've explored how self-love empowers us to find and express our unique voices through advocacy. We've discussed the power of standing up for what we believe in, the challenge of navigating resistance, and the importance of building a supportive community to amplify our efforts. Through advocacy, we can make our mark on the world, contributing to a society that reflects our values, beliefs, and the change we wish to see. It's about using our voices to paint a picture of the world as we believe it can be, one brushstroke at a time.

8.2 THE POWER OF COMMUNITY INVOLVEMENT

The act of contributing to your community does more than just fill an immediate need; it creates connection and shared humanity, reminding us that we're all part of a larger narrative.

Contributing to the Community

Every gesture of kindness, every hour volunteered, and every initiative taken for the betterment of the community sends ripples through society. These actions create a sense of belonging and purpose, anchoring us to our surroundings and to each other. Beyond the visible impact, these contributions nurture a deep sense of fulfillment, illuminating the interconnectedness of our lives. It's akin to planting a garden in a shared space. As you nurture the plants and watch them grow, you're not just cultivating life but fostering a common ground for all to enjoy. Start to engage in activities that brighten the corners where you live. Whether it's organizing a local clean-up, mentoring youth, or starting a community garden, these endeavors enrich the communal soil with growth and beauty.

Finding Your Fit

Discovering where your contributions can have the most impact starts with a reflection on what resonates with you. It's about aligning your passions and values with the needs of the community. This alignment not only ensures that your efforts feel meaningful but also amplifies the impact of your work.

- Explore different avenues for involvement. Local nonprofits, community centers, and social groups often offer a range of opportunities. Attend a few meetings or events to see where you feel most connected.
- Consider your unique skills and interests. Can you offer tutoring in a subject you're passionate about? Does organizing events energize you? Identifying these can guide you to activities where you'll shine.

Learning from Others

Engagement with diverse community members is a rich source of growth and learning. It exposes you to different perspectives and life experiences, broadening your understanding of the world. This diversity enriches your empathy, allowing you to see beyond your viewpoint and appreciate the human experiences that make up your community.

- Initiate conversations with those you meet through your community work. Ask about their stories, listen with an open heart, and share your own. These exchanges are bridges to deeper understanding and connection.
- Be open to learning from everyone, regardless of age, background, or role. Sometimes, the most profound insights come from the most unexpected sources.

Impact on Self-Esteem

Involvement in community work is a mirror reflecting the value of your contributions back at you. It's a powerful affirmation of your ability to effect change and make a difference. This recognition, both from yourself and others bolsters your self-esteem and reinforces the significance of your role in the world.

- Document your experiences and reflections. Write down your community involvement, noting the activities you participated in, the people you met, and the impact you observed. Over time, this record will be a tangible testament to your contributions and growth.
- Celebrate the milestones and achievements of your community work. Did the event you organized raise significant funds? Did the garden you contributed to thrive? Acknowledging these successes strengthens your sense of efficacy and belonging.

In stepping out and contributing to the community, you're not just filling a need or completing a task. You're engaging in a deeply personal act of self-love and respect, affirming your place in the world and your capacity to contribute to its betterment. This involvement is a testament to the power of collective action and the profound impact it can have on both the individual and the community. Through these endeavors, we not only witness but actively participate in the unfolding story of our shared human experience, crafting a narrative of compassion, connection, and growth that enriches us all.

8.3 LEADING WITH LOVE: INSPIRING OTHERS

In a world that often values competition and individual achievement, choosing to lead with love stands out as a pillar of hope and connection. This approach to leadership, grounded in empathy, inclusiveness, and encouragement, not only transforms the way we interact with others but also sets a powerful example that can inspire those around us to adopt similar attitudes and behaviors.

Inspiration through Action

The most profound way to inspire others is through our actions. When we choose to act with love and integrity, we demonstrate that these qualities are not just ideals but practical guides for daily living. This could look like a manager who prioritizes the well-being of their team members, ensuring they feel heard, valued, and supported. Or a teacher who creates an inclusive classroom where every student feels they belong. These actions send a clear message: love and integrity are powerful forces for positive change.

> **Practical Application**: Make a conscious effort to show kindness in small ways throughout your day. Hold the door for someone, offer a word of encouragement, and listen actively when someone is speaking to you. These acts of love, though small, can have a ripple effect, encouraging others to do the same.

Empowering Leadership

Empowering leadership is about uplifting others and enabling them to see and reach their potential. This style of leadership is characterized by empathy, striving to understand the unique perspectives and feelings of others—inclusivity, making sure everyone feels they belong and their contributions are valued, and encouragement, offering support and motivation to help others achieve their best.

Characteristics of Empowering Leaders:

- They listen more than they speak, ensuring everyone's voice is heard.

- They celebrate diversity, recognizing that a range of perspectives enhances creativity and decision-making.
- They provide support and resources for others to grow and succeed.
- They model resilience, showing that setbacks are opportunities for learning and growth.

Creating Positive Change

Each of us has the capacity to create positive change, no matter how small our actions may seem. Whether it's advocating for a cause we believe in, volunteering our time and skills to help those in need, or simply making an effort to be more kind and understanding in our daily interactions, these actions contribute to a larger movement of positivity and love in the world.

Steps to Take Initiative:

- Identify a need in your community that resonates with you. This could be anything from environmental conservation to supporting mental health awareness.
- Research ways you can contribute. This might involve joining an existing organization or starting a new project.
- Take action. Begin with small, manageable steps and gradually expand your efforts as you gain more experience and support.

Legacy of Love

When we lead with love, we leave behind a legacy that outlives our physical presence. This legacy is built on the positive impacts we've had on the lives of others and the example we've set for how to live a life guided by love, empathy, and integrity. It's a legacy that continues to inspire and empower even when we're no longer here, encouraging future generations to carry on the work of making the world a kinder, more inclusive place.

Building Your Legacy:

- Reflect on the values you want to be remembered for. Consider how you can embody these values in your daily actions and interactions.
- Share your knowledge and experiences with others. Mentoring, teaching, and simply sharing stories of your journey can help inspire and guide others.
- Make a commitment to act with love and integrity in all areas of your life. This commitment will be the foundation of your legacy, influencing how you're remembered and the impact you have on the world.

In leading with love, we not only enrich our own lives but also inspire those around us to embrace empathy, inclusiveness, and encouragement. Through our actions, we demonstrate that love is a powerful force for change, capable of transforming communities and building a legacy that continues to positively influence the world. By choosing to lead in this way, we pave the path for others to follow, fostering a cycle of positivity and empowerment that has the potential to reach far beyond our immediate circle.

8.4 ENVIRONMENTAL STEWARDSHIP AS SELF-LOVE

Caring for the planet is a profound expression of self-love. This notion might seem expansive at first glance, but at its core, it's about recognizing that our well-being is deeply entwined with the health of our environment. It's acknowledging that the air we breathe, the water we drink, and the soil that nurtures our food are not just resources but the physical provision for our existence. When we engage in acts of environmental stewardship, we're not only safeguarding the planet for future generations; we're also honoring our place within this intricate web of life.

Connection to the Environment

This connection begins with the simple realization that we are currently part of the natural world. Our bodies and the Earth are composed of the same basic elements, and the rhythms of nature often mirror the cycles within our own lives. This symbiotic relationship suggests that by caring for the Earth, we're also nurturing ourselves. It's like tending to a garden that, in turn, provides us with food, beauty, and solace. By viewing environmental stewardship as an extension of self-love, we start to see conservation and sustainability not as burdens but as acts of kindness toward the planet. Reflect on your daily routines and consider how they connect to the natural world. For example, the water that showers you and the materials that clothe you all come from the Earth. Recognizing these connections can deepen your appreciation for the environment and inspire more mindful living.

Simple Acts of Care

Integrating environmental stewardship into our lives doesn't require grand gestures. Instead, it's the accumulation of small, everyday actions that collectively make a significant impact. These acts of care are as varied as the individuals who perform them, allowing each of us to contribute in ways that resonate with our lives and values.

- Opt for reusable items like water bottles, shopping bags, and straws to minimize waste.
- Support local farmers by buying seasonal produce, reducing the carbon footprint associated with long-distance food transport.
- Conserve energy by turning off lights when not in use and opting for energy-efficient appliances.

By incorporating these simple yet effective practices, we demonstrate respect not only for the environment but also for ourselves as stewards of the planet we call home.

The Ripple Effect

The beauty of individual actions lies in their potential to inspire others. Just as a single pebble can create widespread ripples across a pond, a solitary act of environmental stewardship can encourage a community and even a society to adopt more sustainable habits. This ripple effect amplifies the impact of our actions, transforming personal practices into collective progress.

- Share your environmentally friendly habits on social media or in conversations with friends and family. Your enthusiasm could spark interest and motivate others to make similar changes.
- Organize or participate in local clean-up events. Seeing a group dedicated to caring for a local park or beach can motivate others to join in or start their own initiatives.

Finding Joy in Nature

Immersing ourselves in nature is perhaps the most direct way to connect with the environment and experience the joy it offers.

Whether it's a walk in the park, a hike in the mountains, or simply sitting by a stream, these moments allow us to slow down, breathe, and appreciate the beauty and tranquility of the natural world. This connection nurtures our inner peace, providing a sanctuary for reflection and rejuvenation.

- Make time for regular outdoor activities that you enjoy. Whether it's jogging, biking, or gardening, these moments in nature can be a powerful form of self-care.
- Practice mindfulness in natural settings. Pay attention to the sights, sounds, and smells around you. This presence can deepen your appreciation for the environment and your role in protecting it.

In practicing environmental stewardship, we affirm our love for ourselves and the planet. Through conscious choices, everyday actions, and a heartfelt connection with nature, we honor the intricate bond between our well-being and the health of the Earth. This holistic approach to self-love and environmental care fosters a life that is sustainable, fulfilling, and in harmony with the natural world.

8.5 THE FUTURE OF SELF-LOVE: CONTINUING YOUR JOURNEY

Self-love, much like the ebb and flow of the ocean tides, is a dynamic force that grows and shifts alongside us throughout our lives. It's not a static state of being but a practice that requires nurturing reflection and occasional recalibration to align with our evolving selves and the world around us.

Lifelong Journey

Our self-love practices need to adapt as we journey through different phases of life. From our early childhood all the way up to our later years of life, we can always continue practicing self-love and personal growth. What worked for us at one stage may not serve us in another, and that's perfectly okay. It's a sign of growth. Recognizing and embracing this fluid nature of self-love allows us to remain open to discovering new ways to care for ourselves as we face life's inevitable shifts and turns.

Adapting Self-Love Practices

Adapting our self-love practices is akin to learning a new dance. Initially, it might feel awkward, even frustrating, as we step on our toes trying to find the rhythm. But with patience and practice, we find our flow. This adaptation might mean shifting from high-energy activities to more gentle forms of self-care, changing our social habits, or even reevaluating our goals and what success looks like to us. It's about listening intently to our inner selves and honoring what we hear, even if it means stepping into unfamiliar territory.

- Start by checking in with yourself regularly. Ask, "What do I need at this moment?" The answer could be as simple as a night in or as significant as a career change.
- Be open to exploring new practices. If journaling has lost its spark, perhaps a creative outlet like painting or gardening will reignite your passion for self-expression.
- Remember, there's no one-size-fits-all approach. What matters is that your practices resonate with you and your current circumstances.

Passing on the Message

Sharing the wisdom of self-love is akin to passing on a cherished family recipe, with each person adding their own unique flavor while keeping the essence intact. By sharing our stories and the lessons we've learned, we not only enrich our understanding but also inspire those around us to embark on their own path to self-love. This act of sharing creates a ripple effect, fostering a culture where love, acceptance, and personal growth are celebrated and encouraged.

- Talk about your self-love journey with friends and family. Highlight both the triumphs and the challenges, making it clear that it's a process, not a destination.
- If you're comfortable, use social media or blogging as a platform to share your experiences and connect with others on similar paths.
- Engage in community events or workshops focused on personal development and self-care. Sharing space with like-minded individuals can be both affirming and inspiring.

Vision for the Future

Envisioning a future anchored in self-love invites us to dream of a world where each person recognizes their inherent worth and cultivates a life that reflects their unique essence. In this future, relationships will be grounded in mutual respect and understanding, communities will thrive on the principles of empathy and inclusivity, and the ripple effects of our collective self-love practices will contribute to a more compassionate and vibrant world.

- Imagine a day in your life, years from now, where self-love informs every decision you make, from the work you do to the relationships you nurture. What does that look like?
- Ponder how the world might change if everyone practiced self-love. How would our communities, our environments, and our global society transform?

As we draw this chapter to a close, let us hold onto the understanding that self-love guides us through life's journey with kindness, courage, and an open heart. It's a path that we walk every day, with each step taking us closer to a life filled with joy, fulfillment, and an unwavering sense of our own worth. As we move forward, let's carry this message of love and acceptance with us, sharing its light with the world and shaping a future where self-love is the foundation upon which we build our dreams.

PRACTICAL TOOLS FOR EVERYDAY SELF-LOVE

Remember that every day begins a new day, one that is open to growth, accomplishment, and self-appreciation. The struggles of yesterday are in the past, and you can focus on what's ahead. Think of your daily routine of self-love, adding depth and vibrancy to your day, turning those ordinary moments into something extraordinary. Those morning affirmations or nighttime reflections can set the stage for how each day starts or ends.

9.1 CREATING A SELF-LOVE RITUAL

Establishing Morning Rituals

Morning is the prologue to your day's story. How you start these initial moments can set the tone for the chapters to come. Imagine sipping your favorite warm beverage in silence, not rushing through, but really tasting it, feeling its warmth. This can be a part of your morning ritual. Here's how to craft one:

- Choose Activities That Spark Joy: Maybe it's yoga, maybe it's reading a page from your favorite book, or maybe it's just sitting in silence. Pick what makes you feel good.
- Keep It Simple: Your ritual shouldn't feel like a chore. If five minutes is all you have, use it wisely. A single, mindful breath can be more powerful than an hour lost in hustle.
- Incorporate Affirmations: Start your day by affirming your worth. "Today, I choose to see the best in myself" can be a powerful declaration to set a positive mindset.

Evening Reflections

Evenings are the epilogue of your day. It's a time to wind down, turn the pages back, and reflect on the moments that moved you, challenged you, or brought you joy.

- Gratitude List: Every night, jot down three things you're grateful for. It could be as simple as a delicious meal, a smile from a stranger, or the comfort of your bed.
- Reflect on Achievements: Recognize your accomplishments, no matter their size. Finished a project? Cooked a meal? Did you take time for self-care? Acknowledge it.
- Set Intentions for Tomorrow: Think about what you wish for the next day. Setting intentions can help you move forward with purpose and clarity.

Personalizing Your Rituals

Your self-love rituals should be as unique as you are. They're personal letters of love and care to yourself, written in actions and thoughts.

- Tune Into Your Needs: Some days you might need energy and motivation; other days, you need comfort and calm. Let your rituals evolve with your emotional landscape.
- Experiment: Try out different activities to see what resonates with you. Your morning ritual might be a solo dance party one day and a meditation the next.

Consistency and Flexibility

While rituals thrive on consistency, they also require the flexibility to adapt to life's ever-changing rhythms.

- Create a Habit: Aim to practice your rituals at the same time each day. This consistency helps establish them as nonnegotiable parts of your routine.
- Be Kind to Yourself: There will be days when your rituals might not fit into your schedule, and that's okay. The beauty of self-love is its understanding and forgiveness.

Craft Your Perfect Morning Ritual Quiz

Welcome to the "Craft Your Perfect Morning Ritual" quiz! Answer the following questions to uncover personalized morning rituals that align with your preferences and promote self-love. Let's get started!

Question 1: How do you typically feel when you wake up in the morning?
a) Energetic and ready to conquer the day!
b) Neutral—it depends on the day.
c) Tired and in need of some motivation.

Question 2: What is your preferred way to start your day?
a) A burst of physical activity—exercise or stretching.
b) Sipping a warm beverage while checking emails or news.
c) Taking it slow with a few extra minutes in bed.

Question 3: What type of environment energizes you in the morning?
a) Bright and vibrant colors, lots of natural light.
b) A calm and organized space.
c) Cozy and comfortable, with soft lighting.

Question 4: How do you like to nourish your body in the morning?
a) A hearty and nutritious breakfast.
b) A light and quick snack.
c) Just coffee or tea to start.

Question 5: What activity makes you feel most centered and mindful?
a) Meditation or deep breathing exercises.
b) Reading or journaling.
c) Enjoying a quiet moment in nature.

Results:

Mostly A's: Your perfect morning ritual involves an energizing exercise followed by a nutritious breakfast. Consider incorporating a short meditation for an extra boost of mindfulness.

Mostly B's: You thrive on a balanced and organized start to your day. Sipping a hot drink, checking emails, and spending a few moments in quiet reflection will suit you well.

Mostly C's: A slow and gentle morning is your ideal. Take some extra time in bed, enjoy a cozy environment, and start with a simple, warm beverage.

Congratulations! You've crafted your perfect morning ritual. Feel free to incorporate these personalized suggestions into your daily routine and embrace the self-love that comes with starting your day on a positive note.

By weaving self-love into the fabric of your daily routines, you transform them into rituals of care and appreciation for yourself. These rituals, both morning and evening, are not just tasks to be checked off but are acts of kindness toward yourself, reminders of your worth, and affirmations of your ability to face each day with a heart full of love.

9.2 THE IMPORTANCE OF SELF-REFLECTION JOURNALS

In the quiet moments of the day, when the world slows down, and we find ourselves alone with our thoughts, a golden opportunity presents itself. It's in these moments that the act of journaling transforms from a simple pastime to a profound tool for self-discovery. We've discussed journaling throughout this book, and now it's time to be sure we put it into practice. Through the gentle flow of ink on paper, we begin to peel back the layers of our consciousness, revealing the intricate feelings, thoughts, and desires that make us uniquely who we are.

Journaling for Self-Discovery

The beauty of journaling lies in its simplicity and accessibility. With just a notebook and a pen, you unlock a safe space for introspection and exploration. This process of self-discovery invites you to ask and answer questions you might not have considered before. What truly brings you joy? What fears hold you back? How do you define success on your own terms? Each entry serves as a snapshot of your internal landscape at a given moment, providing insights into the depths of your psyche.

Structured Prompts

To guide you on this voyage of self-discovery, consider these structured prompts as your map. They're designed to gently nudge you toward deeper reflection, helping you uncover truths about yourself and the world around you:

- Today, I felt most alive when …
- A fear I'm ready to let go of is …
- I feel most like myself when …
- One thing I learned about myself today is …
- A situation I handled well/not so well today was … because …

These prompts are starting points. Feel free to let your thoughts wander where they will, following the natural flow of your reflections.

Regular Review

The true magic of journaling unfolds over time. Regularly reviewing your entries allows you to track your evolution, highlighting patterns in your feelings and behaviors. Perhaps you'll notice that certain situations consistently trigger anxiety or that particular activities bring you disproportionate joy. This awareness is the first step toward making intentional changes in your life, guiding you toward more of what nurtures your soul and away from what depletes it.

- Make it a habit to review your journal entries once a month or even once a season. Look for recurring themes or shifts in your perspective.
- Reflect on the progress you've made toward your goals and the obstacles you've encountered. How have you grown from these experiences?

Privacy and Honesty

For your journal to be a true tool of self-discovery, it must be a place of uninhibited honesty. This level of openness requires a guarantee of privacy. Only in knowing that your thoughts are for your eyes alone can you feel free to explore the most vulnerable corners of your heart and mind without fear of judgment.

- Consider keeping your journal in a private, secure place. If you're concerned about privacy, you might even develop a simple code for particularly sensitive entries. Make sure the boundaries around your journal are known to those who could potentially have access.
- Remind yourself regularly that your journal is a judgment-free zone. The goal is not to critique your thoughts or feelings but to understand them.

The act of journaling, then, is much more than a mere diary of daily events. It's an intimate dance with the self, a way to record the melody of your inner voice and the rhythm of your evolving story. Through the pages of your journal, you chart the course of your personal growth, navigating the waters of self-discovery with curiosity, openness, and an unwavering commitment to understanding the depths of your being. In this way, each entry becomes a stepping stone on your path, a testament to the journey of becoming who you are meant to be.

9.3 BUILDING A PERSONAL SUPPORT NETWORK

A myriad of faces, voices, and hearts that stand by you, uplift you, and propel you forward—this is the essence of a personal support network. It's not merely about having people in your life; it's about fostering connections with those who energize you, cheer for your victories, and offer a shoulder during the inevitable lows.

Identifying Supportive People

Spotting those gems in your life that can form the bedrock of your support network involves tuning into subtle cues and actions. It's the friend who texts to ask how your day went, the mentor who offers constructive criticism with warmth, or the family member who celebrates your quirks. These individuals radiate positivity, encourage your dreams, and respect your boundaries.

- Pay attention to how you feel after spending time with someone. Do you feel uplifted, understood, and energized? These are signs of a supportive connection.
- Look for consistency in their support. True support isn't fleeting; it's steady and reliable through both the mundane days and the pivotal moments.

Cultivating Connections

Once you've identified the supportive figures in your life, the next step is to deepen these connections. This involves more than the occasional catch-up or shared activity; it's about nurturing these relationships with intention and care.

- Make an effort to communicate regularly. This doesn't mean daily texts or calls, but checking in with each other frequently enough to stay updated on each other's lives.
- Engage in activities that enrich your bond. This could be a shared hobby, a mutual interest in a particular cause, or simply regular meet-ups to chat and unwind.
- Be there for them as they are for you. Support is a two-way street. Show up for their important moments, offer help when they're in need, and listen with empathy and without judgment.

Support Groups and Communities

Beyond individual connections, tapping into the collective wisdom and strength of support groups and communities can amplify your self-love journey. These groups, whether online or in person, bring together individuals with shared experiences, challenges, or goals, offering a space for mutual encouragement, learning, and growth.

- Research groups that align with your interests or challenges. This could be a book club, a fitness group, a support group for a specific personal challenge, or an online community focused on personal development.
- Participate actively once you join. Share your experiences, ask questions, and offer your insights or support to others. Active participation not only helps you gain more from the group but also strengthens the community as a whole.
- Respect the dynamics and rules of the group. Each community has its own ethos and guidelines. Honoring

these helps maintain a positive, supportive environment for all members.

Giving Back

The beauty of a support network lies not just in what you receive but also in what you give. Contributing to your support network reinforces a culture of mutual care and appreciation. It's about recognizing that every act of support you offer not only uplifts someone else but also enriches your life, creating a cycle of positivity that strengthens the bonds within your network.

- Offer your skills or knowledge. If you have expertise in a particular area, offer to help others in your network who could benefit from it. This could be as simple as helping a friend with a resume or sharing advice on a topic you're knowledgeable about.
- Celebrate others' successes. Make it a point to acknowledge and celebrate the achievements of those in your network. A congratulatory message, a small gift, or simply sharing in their joy can mean a lot.
- Be a source of positivity. Strive to be someone others can turn to for encouragement and a positive perspective. Sometimes, a hopeful outlook or a kind word can be the most powerful support you can offer.

In building your personal support network, remember that each connection adds strength, warmth, and color to your life. It's a living, evolving entity that mirrors the care, intention, and love you invest in it. Through identifying supportive people, deepening these connections, engaging with supportive groups, and giving back, you cultivate a network that not only supports you through life's journey but also enriches your journey with shared laughter, learning, and love.

9.4 EMBRACING CHANGE AND GROWTH WITH LOVE

Change, often cloaked in uncertainty, can unsettle the most steadfast hearts. Yet, within its folds lies the potential for remarkable transformation, a chance to bloom anew. Learning to welcome change with open arms invites a world of possibilities, nurturing an environment where personal growth isn't just possible but thrives.

Viewing Change Positively

The initial wave of change can feel like a cold gust on a warm day, unexpected and jarring. However, shifting our mindset to perceive change as a catalyst for growth turns this breeze into a refreshing wind, guiding us toward new horizons. Recognizing change as an inherent part of life's rhythm encourages us to ride its waves with curiosity and optimism, eager to discover where they might lead.

- Embrace change as an opportunity for self-discovery. Each new situation presents a chance to learn more about our strengths, desires, and resilience.
- Celebrate the flexibility that change brings. It teaches us to adapt, fostering a spirit of versatility that serves us in all of life's endeavors.

Growth Mindset

Adopting a growth mindset transforms obstacles into stepping stones, challenges, and lessons. This perspective champions the belief that our abilities and intelligence can be developed through dedication and hard work. It's a testament to the power of perseverance, a promise that every effort contributes to our journey of becoming.

- View challenges as opportunities to expand your knowledge and skills. Every hurdle overcome is a victory, a testament to your growing capabilities.
- Cultivate patience and persistence. Progress might be slow, but with consistent effort, improvement is inevitable.

Self-Love in Transition

Times of transition, marked by change and uncertainty, demand a special kind of self-love. It's during these periods that maintaining our self-care rituals and leaning on our support networks become crucial, providing stability amid the flux.

- Hold onto your self-care practices as anchors. Whether it's a morning walk or an evening of reading, these rituals offer solace and continuity.
- Reach out to your support network for encouragement and perspective. Friends, family, and mentors can offer invaluable guidance and reassurance during uncertain times.

Celebrating Evolution

Reflecting on our growth and evolution is a practice steeped in self-love. It acknowledges the journey we've undertaken, the hurdles we've navigated, and the person we've become. This celebration is not just about reaching a destination but also honoring the path we've traveled and the transformation we've undergone.

- Regularly set aside time to reflect on your personal growth. Acknowledge the changes within you, the lessons learned, and the strengths gained.
- Share your growth journey with others. Your story can inspire and motivate, reminding those around you of the beauty inherent in change and evolution.

In navigating the landscapes of change and growth, we find that embracing them with love and optimism opens doors to uncharted territories of self-discovery and development. It's in these moments of transition that our true potential is tested, and often, it's where we shine brightest. By viewing change positively, fostering a growth mindset, caring for ourselves through transitions, and celebrating our evolution, we not only adapt to the world around us but also shape it with our unique colors and textures.

As we move forward, let us carry with us the lessons gleaned from these experiences, the resilience forged in the face of change, and the joy found in personal growth. In doing so, we pave the way for a future rich with possibility, ready to embrace whatever comes next with open hearts and minds. Put into practice everything that we've learned, and you'll be able to stand up and proclaim, "I'm proud of me being me!"

CONCLUSION

As we reach the closing pages of our journey together, it's essential to pause and reflect on the transformative power of self-love. This book has been a testament to the undeniable truth that self-love is not a mere luxury but a cornerstone necessity for you, the teen girls navigating the complexities of adolescence. It's the foundation upon which healthy relationships, mental well-being, and personal growth are built.

Through these chapters, you've embarked on a profound journey of self-discovery. From understanding the essence of self-love to integrating practical strategies into your daily life, each step has been a move toward embracing the unique, wonderful person you are. We've explored creating self-love rituals, fostering positive self-talk, setting realistic goals, navigating social media with a positive mindset, and building networks of support that uplift and empower.

Remember, self-love is an ongoing journey that flourishes with persistence, patience, and practice. The tools and strategies we've shared are not just for today but for all the tomorrows to come as you grow and encounter new experiences and challenges. I encourage you to keep these tools close, revisiting them as often as needed, allowing them to guide you as you evolve.

I also invite you to be an advocate for self-love, not just for yourself but among your peers. Share the knowledge and insights you've gained, creating a ripple effect of positivity and empowerment. Your journey and successes with self-love can inspire and encourage others, fostering a community where self-love is celebrated and nurtured.

Your potential for growth and impact is boundless. As you practice self-love, remember that your personal development contributes to a more compassionate, understanding world. We are all interconnected, and your journey of self-love has the power to touch the lives of those around you in profound ways.

I would be honored to hear about your journey and successes with self-love. Whether you choose to share your story on social media, with friends, or even back with me, know that your experiences can contribute to a thriving community of support and encouragement.

Lastly, allow me to leave you with these words of encouragement and empowerment: You are worthy, strong, and resilient. The journey of self-love you're on is a beautiful, transformative process that leads to discovering the best version of yourself. You are not alone in this journey. With the insights and strategies from this book, self-love is now within your reach more than ever.

Embrace your journey with an open heart, and remember, the most extraordinary relationship you will ever have is the one you have with yourself. Here's to a future where you shine brightly, fueled by the unwavering power of self-love.

REFERENCES

13 Ways to Boost Your Daughter's Self-Esteem https://childmind.org/article/13-ways-to-boost-your-daughters-self-esteem/

150 Journaling Prompts for Self-Discovery in the New Year https://parade.com/health/journaling-prompts-for-self-discovery

16 Environmental Activities for Students to Encourage ... https://www.teachstarter.com/us/blog/environmental-activities-for-students-sustainability-classroom/

21 Family Bonding Activities to Strengthen Your ... https://selfsufficientkids.com/family-bonding-activities/

21 Mindfulness Exercises & Activities For Adults (+ PDF) https://positivepsychology.com/mindfulness-exercises-techniques-activities/

4 Steps to Help Your Teen Overcome Setbacks https://www.mytutor.co.uk/blog/parents/4-steps-to-help-your-teen-overcome-setbacks/

Assertiveness (for Teens) - Nemours KidsHealth https://kidshealth.org/en/teens/assertive.html

Be the One: Six True Stories of Teens Overcoming ... https://www.chconline.org/resourcelibrary/one-six-true-stories-teens-overcoming-hardship-hope/

Communication Skills for You and Your Family https://www.udel.edu/canr/cooperative-extension/fact-sheets/comunications-skills-your-family/

Developing Leadership Skills Among Adolescents and ... https://www.tandfonline.com/doi/full/10.1080/02673843.2017.1292928

Effect of breathwork on stress and mental health: A meta- ... https://www.nature.com/articles/s41598-022-27247-y

Five Benefits of Teen Volunteering https://www.unitedwayhelps.org/blog/5-benefits-of-teen-volunteering

Food for Thought: Healthy Nutrition in Teens Effects Mood and Emotional Health https://www.viewpointcenter.com/food-for-thought-healthy-nutrition-in-teens-effects-mood-and-emotional-health/#:.

Forgiving Family: Setting Healthy Boundaries - Centerstone https://centerstone.org/our-resources/health-wellness/forgiving-family-setting-healthy-boundaries/

Healthy Routine For Teenagers - Why It's Important https://www.sparktheirfuture.qld.edu.au/why-routines-matter-for-growing-teenage-brains/#:

How Self-Compassion Can Improve Teen Mental Health https://www.psychologytoday.com/us/blog/the-mindful-teen/202301/how-self-compassion-can-improve-teen-mental-health

How to Help Teens Set Effective Goals (Tips & Templates) https://biglifejournal.com/blogs/blog/guide-effective-goal-setting-teens-template-worksheet

How to Help Your Teen Manage Toxic Friendships https://riveroakspsychology.com/how-to-help-your-teen-manage-toxic-friendships/#:

How to Set Boundaries With Your Family | TIME https://time.com/6331383/how-to-set-boundaries-family/

How to Teach Positive Self-Talk https://www.thepathway2success.com/how-to-teach-positive-self-talk/

How Using Social Media Affects Teenagers https://childmind.org/article/how-using-social-media-affects-teenagers/

Mindfulness for Teens: Benefits and Practice Tips https://psychcentral.com/health/the-benefits-of-mindfulness-meditation-for-teens

Mobilising Social Support to Improve Mental Health for ... https://www.ncbi.nlm.nih.gov/pmc/articles/PMC8136658/

Peer Pressure: Strategies to Help Teens Handle it Effectively https://parentandteen.com/handle-peer-pressure/

Physical Activity and Mental Health: What is the Connection? https://www.massgeneral.org/children/physical-activity/mental-health

Root of Teen Empathy Begins with Secure Relationships at ... https://www.cnn.com/2021/07/15/health/teen-empathy-secure-family-relationships-wellness/index.html

Self-advocacy: helping teenagers speak up for themselves https://raisingchildren.net.au/teens/development/social-emotional-development/self-advocacy-helping-teenagers-speak-up-for-themselves

Setting Healthy Boundaries with Your Teen https://www.embarkbh.com/blog/the-importance-of-setting-healthy-boundaries-with-your-teen/

Social Media and Youth Mental Health https://www.hhs.gov/surgeongeneral/priorities/youth-mental-health/social-media/index.html

Social Media and Youth Mental Health https://www.hhs.gov/surgeongeneral/priorities/youth-mental-health/social-media/index.html

Stress Management and Teens https://www.aacap.org/AACAP/Families_and_Youth/Facts_for_Families/FFF-Guide/Helping-Teenagers-With-Stress-066.aspx

Teenagers and communication https://www.betterhealth.vic.gov.au/health/healthyliving/teenagers-and-communication

The Importance of Goal-Setting for Teens https://bgca.org/news-stories/2022/January/the-importance-of-goal-setting-for-teens#:

The Importance of Spotting Teen Strengths https://www.chop.edu/news/health-tip/importance-spotting-teen-strengths

Why Celebrating Successes is Important to Our Mental Health https://innovativeresources.org/why-celebrating-successes-is-important-to-our-mental-health/

Why Sleep is Important for Teens | Johns Hopkins Medicine https://www.hopkinsmedi cine.org/all-childrens-hospital/services/pediatric-and-adolescent-medicine/ healthy-weight-initiative/ages-12-17/why-sleep-is-important-for-teens#:

www.ingramcontent.com/pod-product-compliance
Lightning Source LLC
Chambersburg PA
CBHW070715130626
46553CB00005B/2003